One Hand
Alone
Cannot Clap

An Arab Israeli Universe

Greville Janner

Robson Books

First published in Great Britain in 1998 by Robson Books Ltd.,
Bolsover House, 5–6 Clipstone Street, London W1P 8LE

British Library Cataloguing in Publication Data
A catalogue record for this title is available from the British Library

ISBN 1 86105 217 0

Printed in Great Britain by
WBC Books Manufacturers Ltd., Bridgend.
Mid-Glamorgan

IN MEMORY OF
MYRA

AND FOR
OUR GRANDCHILDREN:
ISABEL, ESTHER AND PHOEBE
TALI, NATAN AND ELLA AVIGAIL

THAT THEY MAY GROW UP IN A WORLD OF
PEACE

FOREWORD

BY SHIMON PERES

Greville Janner, a serious person who plays important roles both in his own country, the United Kingdom, and among his Jewish people, has also kept a small nook of mischief for himself by adding the art of magic to his versatile talents. In his heart, he knows that there is no greater magic for children than a magician with the gift to spark their imagination.

By means of this book, we discover anew that Greville is not only capable of performing magic, but also of falling under its spell.

I do not know whether it is harder to cast a spell or to be under its influence. For although one can learn how to become a magician, the capacity of being magic-stricken is of a much deeper nature and, I would even venture to say, an uncommon quality in today's world. A world so full of contradictions, disappointments, and impotence. A world in which the diary holding the entries of a man's life-chronicle consists of pages which are successively torn out, and are lost in an abyss from which there is no return. In a world such as this, to act under the influence of a charm is to bring forth a smile on a child's lips, brighten up a face, discover a wild flower amidst a field of thorns, and experience a sudden surge of kinship in an otherwise indifferent environment.

To be touched by magic, you have to be magnanimous. To

1

generate generosity in others, you must first start by being generous yourself. And this, indeed, is the essence of Greville Janner. He crosses continents and oceans. He meets heads of state and converses with ordinary people. He beholds landscapes and has become proficient in many languages, and through all of these experiences he has sought, and discovered afresh, a beam of light sufficient for him to start afresh with a new dawn in his heart.

To be a magician, or to be bewitched, does not necessarily mean that one does not experience deep sorrow. This kind of profound grief struck Greville Janner when his beloved wife and life companion, Myra, died.

He sought a place in which to hide, so that his grief would not sadden others. And thus, in his own distinctive fashion, his footsteps led him to a large Arab settlement in the north of Israel, Sakhnin. He wanted to experience life in the village in order to learn a new language, Arabic, breathe a different air, that of Upper Galilee, get to know the mode of thought of another people, the Arabs, and be in a position to compare what he had heard and that which he knew, with the flow of everyday reality.

From the first moment, he was charmed by the family who were the proprietors of the Shadi Guest House. In his book, he makes no attempt to conceal the fact that the streets of the village are run-down or to ignore the mosquito-bites at night; but simultaneously, he discovers the strength and charm of an Arab family, which continues to live there with unflagging tenacity, in a genuine effort to resist the lure of all the temptations of this new world – a family that fiercely safeguards the special brand of loyalty which characterizes the Hamoula – the extended family.

As far as they are concerned, the world is not a global village; for them, the village is a global world. And in this village, he discovers a measure of hospitality which is unequalled. He is accepted in their midst as a member of the family. They are solicitous of how he spends his time, concerned with what he eats and with the way he feels.

In spite of the fact that they were as surprised by him as he by them – a current of uncommon closeness draws them to each other, with unexpected revelations. The most amazing of them all is that we are all fashioned from the same matter and, as opposed to the general belief, that we have not been brought into this world to wage war one against the other, but to live with one another as guests and neighbours. He feels at home while he is nursing his personal grief; the unfamiliarity sensed stems from the distance between them, and the goodwill from the proximity.

This is no ordinary book. It exposes, in good spirit and without pretension, real circumstance – like an excellent novel which reveals that behind the thick veils of our lives lies the hope of magic: the hope that lives within magicians and in those under their spell.

INTRODUCTION

You need two hands to clap, but only one shared tongue to communicate. For my work on the ups and downs of the Middle East Peace Process and for my pleasure in sharing with Arab friends what we hold in common, that tongue had to be Arabic. To learn it meant immersing myself in the Arab world. This is the story of that immersion, in the Lower Galilee, Israel Arab town of Sakhnin.

Israel's foes have long regarded me as Israel's parliamentary voice. As a Jewish MP, peer, Zionist leader and one time President of the Board of Deputies of British Jews, I have always regarded that as a proud role – to ensure that Israel's case is heard in Britain's Parliament and beyond. But equally, I have always believed that if Jews are to live at peace in the Middle East and hence in the world at large, they can only do so by making peace, with their neighbours. For Israel that meant and means – the Arab world.

So I joined in founding the Maimonides Foundation – a unique organization which fosters close and good relations between Muslims and Jews, both in Britain and in the wider world. Working from that platform and as a Member of the House of Commons, as opposed to the Knesset, I was received with courtesy, kindness and respect in many Arab lands, in the Middle East, the Gulf and North Africa. Curiously though, until now, I had never even considered entering that part of the Arab world which lives within the borders of the Jewish State. That, combined

5

with my irritation at my inability to communicate with Arabs in their own tongue, led me to my linguistic and humanistic adventure in Sakhnin.

My study of Arabic began with two BBC audio tapes of Egyptian Arabic. Then Douglas Krikler – Director of the Maimonides Foundation, and my friend – created a world of personalized audio tapes for me, making my car journeys a pleasure. But our working communications were urgent and although he taught me that 'Allah is with those who are patient', his patience did not stretch to conversations with me in Arabic, at much the speed at which his tiny daughter talks English with him. So it was tape after tape of essential Arabic.

We found that Arabic proverbs went down well with Arab friends and listeners. The unclapped, lonely hand came in Douglas's second batch. To my delight, King Hassan of Morocco quoted the proverb, in his Rabat Palace, during his introduction to a group of us from the Board of Deputies of British Jews. You need two parties for a peace process. '*Yad wahida la tusafiq*' – one hand alone cannot clap.

So it was to help provide a second hand – a Jewish hand – to clap, that I decided to soak myself in the language, culture and lifestyle of our Israeli Arab cousins. And to hope that it might help just a little to keep both hands clapping, especially when the tempo is grim.

It was one of my friends who said: 'Why don't you write a book about it?' I said: 'Who'll read it?' She said: 'Lots of people. I will, anyway.'

I asked myself: should I *really* write this book? I took out a pad and jotted down some pros and cons.

First: Abdullah and family at the Shadi Guest House in Sakhnin. *Pro the book*: the world will know that they are marvellous and it will be a solid token of my gratitude for the hospitality received and appreciated. *Con the book*: they have made me so patently welcome. Will the book make *them* unwelcome, anywhere that they care about?

6

Solution: ask Abdullah what he thinks about the book. I did. He said it would be wonderful.

Second: will it help or harm my work in the field of Jewish-Arab relations if I put my very frank thoughts onto paper?

Pro the book: it should create interest and goodwill and I hope be read in the spirit in which I wrote it – as a very personal contribution to understanding the joys of diversity. *Con the book*: the Maimonides Foundation has, in the main, worked quietly and discreetly, believing that what matters are personal relationships, which are often delicate and can dissolve in print. Words on paper might be misconstrued and would offend where no offence is intended. And a gentleman is a man who never intentionally offends.

Solution: ask Douglas. I did and he said: 'If you have something to say, then say it. But with care.'

Third: in the past, I have always written books about the law or presentational skills, avoiding personal anecdote and opinion. Will this book be regarded, then, as an ego trip? Worse, will it upset my family, when I write about (for instance) the impact of this visit on our shared bereavement and my way of coping with it?

Pro the book: when I was first elected to Parliament, a wise old man called Bernard (later Lord) Braine, came up and put his arm around my shoulder. 'Welcome to the Commons, my boy,' he said. 'Your father and I were on opposite sides of the House for many years but we were always friends. I hope that we will be.'

'I would be honoured to be your friend, Bernard,' I replied. 'As a veteran parliamentarian, have you any advice for me?' 'Yes,' said Bernard. 'Never do good by stealth!' Which sounded a little like the Machiavellian dictum: be seen to do good deeds but delegate unpopular decisions to others.

You may win a campaign by deliberate silence but you can rarely influence opinion by keeping yours to yourself. In political terms, you will not get re-elected unless your electorate knows of your good deeds. Well, I am not standing for re-election. But I want others to know the good deeds of the Halayle family, and to join in the quest for the truly Holy Grail of goodwill.

Con the book: I would really prefer to write this book for family posterity, rather than for public reading. If the book is going to be real, then I must record my feelings. Or maybe not? First solution: keep my own views out of it. Just describe, explain and let my readers make up their own minds.

On clear balance, and as will be blindingly obvious, I decided to write this book. I did it first, omitting my views. Friends and colleagues whose opinions I value, all said: it is too descriptive. Not enough depth. It is not good enough to record what other people told you. You must give your reactions.

Al Fadi Yaamel Qadi – the idle one makes himself a judge. I must not be a mere armchair critic – one who criticizes, without getting involved. My colleagues told me that enduring a life-time of involvement had qualified me to speak my mind. My faults do not include idleness and I must have the courage to take a view and to express it.

So I rewrote and expanded the book and behold, for better, I hope – or for worse, maybe – you have here the benefit of my well-considered bias.

In Sakhnin, I had time for thought, and it was an excellent discipline to put those thoughts firmly onto the record. If they help towards harmony and bring useful results, in my lifetime, so much the better. Anyway, my grandchildren may enjoy catching a glimpse of my mind. Maybe my thoughts may spur them to work for the causes that dominate my public life – not least, the search for human harmony. The Shadi Guest House would make an excellent start for them as it was a continuation for me. It was there that I first talked Arabic, most of each day. But it is not enough to learn a language. You must also be careful to whom you speak it.

During the 1992 General Election, I kept passing the Cypriot Kebab House, on a main Leicester street. I called out to them in my best Greek: '*Yasu, yasu*' – hello. They would come to the door and wave and shout back: '*Yasu*'. I would then call: '*Efkharisto*' – thank you. They would wave again.

8

Shortly after the election, a man came to one of my surgeries, my advice sessions. 'Do you remember me?' I am from the Cyprus Kebab House, on the Narborough Road.'

'Of course I remember you,' I explained. 'Did you like it when I came by and said "*Yasu*", and "*Efkharisto*"?'

'No,' he replied.

'Why not?'

'Because we are Turkish!'

At least in Sakhnin I knew that they were laughing either at me or at my Arabic and not because I was talking to them in someone else's language. They took me into their *hamoula* – their extended family – and made me feel at home in their home. I will always be grateful to them all. As I am to my friends in the Maimonides Foundation; to my daughters Laura and Marion; my son-in-law, David; to Douglas Krikler and to Jon Mendelson, for so carefully reading and so helpfully criticizing my manuscript – and, above all, to my dear friend Shimon Peres for his kindly and perceptive Foreword.

Chapter One

IN THE BEGINNING

Bﾠritish friends called it, crazy ... pleasantly mad ... or, perhaps, just a little eccentric. Some Arabs said: '*Majnoon*', and pointed to their heads. But to me, to stay in a small Arab town, in a largely Arab area of the Jewish State, was a new and formative experience. Part of the motive was to live in and to study a sister civilization and language; part of the road to new experiences in a very old world; part a joyful return to the realities of my youth.

My first, lone language journey was in Spain in 1948. I was twenty years old and just out of the British army. I spent a week in what was then a village – Laredo, on the north coast. In school, I had learned the essentials of Spanish. In Laredo, I learned how Spaniards speak it. In the little hotel and in the bars . . . out with the fishermen, at sea, where they were not afraid to tell me precisely what they thought of Franco's government, and in spectacular language . . . on the evening parade, when the villagers walked up and down – what they called '*dar paseos*'. I learned how

Spanish youngsters used the language to 'pluck the turkey' – to 'chat up the birds'.

I gave some English lessons in the local school, run by two Franciscan monks – la Escuela de los Dos Frailes. My lessons were not very good, but the children loved the songs and the magic that I taught them with such enthusiasm. In return, they taught me Spanish and pelota.

Now, my wife Myra – '*mushtaraka hayati*', my companion for life – had died. I had retired from the House of Commons. I was free to roam into another world and certainly in a way that Myra would not have wanted to share. So I decided to go to some Arab village, somewhere, and just to live and talk and learn, as I had done so long ago, in Laredo.

I needed a place where I would be forced to speak Arabic. Douglas Krikler had given me a grounding in the language based on the classical tongue – *fus'ha*. I could understand everything I said and some people could sometimes understand me too – but I could never understand what they said in reply.

I thought of Lord (Tom) Denning's classic advice: 'You should always ask yourself questions. We judges always do that. It's the only way we can be sure of getting swift and intelligent answers!' I asked myself the question: where should I go?

Then I asked Douglas. Together with him, and largely on the business of the Maimonides Foundation, with its significant input into fostering of relations between Muslims, Arabs and Jews, I had visited most Arab countries that were prepared to receive me.

That excluded Iraq, Libya and Algeria. I had been almost everywhere else, including an amazing journey to the Yemen, with a group of parliamentarians, and with Jon Mendelsohn, who at that time headed and directed the staff and organizations with which I worked, with loyal and discreet energy.

We travelled through Yemen's strange and wonderful land, in many ways unchanged from the days of the Patriarchs. Some 1400 Jews lived there – in peace, but scarcely in equality, and always at some risk. Many of the men, brilliant silversmiths. All of the community, firm in their traditional faith. A fabled country, but not ideal for my purpose.

Maybe Morocco? I had visited that Arab land, three times. It has some 15,000 Jews, with synagogues and complete freedom to practise their religion. A king to whom they are totally loyal, and who is their friend: leaders, with access to high authority.

On a recent Board of Deputies journey, we were not only received in audience by King Hassan, but we took part in a *Hiloula* – a visit to the shrine of a saintly rabbi, on the Jewish festival of Lag Baomer, with thousands of guests, mainly Jewish, kissing the tombstone of Rabbi Yahya, enjoying the music and the six-course, hundred per cent kosher meal under the huge awning. Maybe *they* had a village that would be pleased to see me?

Or Tunisia? Two visits there, the first one in the days when the Peace Process was doing well and we were received at the very top level. More lately, when the process was on the skids, they were still courteously friendly, but our reception was definitely down-graded.

Never mind – I could go to the extraordinary Tunisian island of Djerba, where some 500 Jews inhabit a village and live their religious lives as in happy days of yore, a reminder of that Golden Age of the Jewish people, in Arab lands. We had been with them when they prepared the Festival of Succoth, building their tabernacles out of leafy boughs, festooned with fresh fruit – in the courtyards of their houses – and spreading their hospitality. We were made most hugely welcome.

Saudi? No Jews. Still standing far back from the Peace Process. Not the place. Douglas, my son Daniel, and I were among the first Zionist Jews to make a semi-official visit to that unique land. But distance in both culture and miles ruled it out for my present project.

What, then, of Syria, with its ancient history, its Jewish community of some 250 souls and its position on the edge of the Peace Process?

I thought over our visit. To the ancient synagogue of the

prophet Elijah – Eliyahu Hanavi. Its grotto, hacked out of the rock. There, by tradition, the Prophet found refuge. The tube cut into the stone, through which they dropped down his food. The ivory stump, the remains of the Prophet's chair. It was draped with a woman's dress. Childless Syrian Jewish women still believe that prayer to the Prophet and a dress on his throne will bring fertility.

There is another fine synagogue, in downtown Damascus. The community can stay or leave as it wishes. But it is ageing. Few Jewish leaders have visited the country or its Jewish community. Especially, few Zionists. We were made greatly welcome. Still, there is an element of danger there. I would not be relaxed. No.

Jordan was a definite possibility. There, we had all felt at home. Myra did not want to visit Amman. She thought it would be dirty and dangerous. It was neither and she loved it. Amman is a clean, modern, friendly city. Pink Petra, with its temples carved out of the rock, is sensational. From palace to refugee camp, we were treated with courteous kindness.

So I returned. Twice, lately, at the invitation of Crown Prince Hassan, to discuss how best to create a World Parliamentary Council against Islamophobia, in the image of our Inter-Parliamentary Council Against Antisemitism. A great man: like his brother, the King – that great survivor.

In 1980, I was received by President Sadat of Egypt. He confidently predicted the overthrow of King Hussein, the downfall of the Saudi dynasty, the collapse of Assad of Syria and of Ghadafi of Libya. All are still there. Only Sadat has gone.

I mulled over those amazing visits to the Arab world, to countries which – until the late Yitzhak Rabin and my friend Shimon Peres opened up the Middle East Peace Process – had been bolted, sealed and shut off from my life as a British Labour MP, and above all, as a Jewish, Zionist leader, I had always regarded Arab countries as unsafe: if not as enemies, then certainly not as friends. Jordan was the most likely.

My daughter Laura had married an Israeli and was settled in Jerusalem. In West Jerusalem, of course. The Peace Process had opened all our horizons, broadened our minds, kindled our hopes. I telephoned David, Laura's husband in Jerusalem. He worked for the American Joint Distribution Committee, as an economic planner, helping both Arab and Jewish development towns to plot their future.

'Why not do it here in Israel?' he asked. 'I'm sure that I can find a place in one of our Arab towns where you could have a very happy time.'

Yes, Israel was a great idea. How strange that I had spent so many months of my life in that country, but how ironic that I knew so little of its Arabs, its Muslim citizens. I have been there so often and I have never met them.

Surely Israel's Arabs should be playing a pivotal role in the quest for peace. As catalysts. They and their Jewish fellow citizens have so much in common – including not only their present but their destiny.

Yet perhaps Israeli Jews and Arabs suspect each other out of shared and unnecessary ignorance. Yes, if David can find me the right place, I will go.

He did. The town of Sakhnin – some 20,000 souls. Large enough to be interesting and yet small enough to have a community life. And bed and breakfast in a private guest house, run by a school teacher and his wife. With a shower and loo, en suite – excellent.

I knew that the great medieval sage, Moses Maimonides, would approve of my visit to Sakhnin. He was born in Spain, where the Jews enjoyed what is still called their 'Golden Age', under the relatively benevolent and brotherly semitic Muslim rule – an age which was snapped to a cruel end by a Catholic kingdom. In 1159 or thereabouts, Maimonides – or Ibn Maimun, as the Arabs called him moved to Fez, in Morocco. I had visited his ancient house, still preserved in his memory.

Then he travelled to Egypt, where he became personal doctor to Saladin. In Muslim Cairo, he wrote *Guide for the Perplexed*, still a definitive work of Jewish and of world philosophy. From Cairo, he answered theological questions from Jewish communities throughout North Africa and the Arab world. When we visited the Yemen, we were shown translations of a letter from Maimonides to Yemeni Jews.

My Sakhnin visit is a small step in his footsteps. The Jewish world should learn from his life and work among our Muslim brothers and sisters.

Another great Moses – Montefiore – was my 19th-century predecessor as President of the Board of Deputies. He was a totally different character. A friend of Queen Victoria, he used his British base to protect and succour Jews in danger anywhere in the Jewish world.

In 1948, my father visited Aden in the wake of vicious anti-Jewish riots. At that time, Aden was a British Protectorate and my father was a British MP. As a result of his visit, Britain granted visas to hundreds of Adenese Jews, who formed the nucleus of what is today the small but distinguished Adenese Jewish community in London.

People sometimes ask me why I am so involved in work for the Jewish people and I tell them that it is an hereditary disease. I would like to think that in some small way, the inheritance stretches back, beyond my father, to the two men called Moses.

Still (I mused), why visit Sakhnin when I could spend the week (for instance) seeking remnants of Holocaust gold, for survivors of Nazi persecution and their heirs? Lithuanians in the Nazi mould had herded many of my family into a synagogue, set light to it and burned them to death. I had searched for the remains of others in our ancestral Latvian and Lithuanian villages. All I had found were mass graves.

Add the memories of the children in the post-war Bergen Belsen Jewish Children's Home, and I start to unravel my motives. The children sang in Hebrew: 'I am going to The Land, with songs and with joy'. But the Bevinite British Government blocked their way and they were stranded in that long, low, former

German army barrack.

So I had become a Zionist. In 1948, my friends and I had danced the *hora* in Trafalgar Square when the UN accepted Israel's statehood. For over a quarter of a century I had pleaded the cause of the Jewish State, in season and out of season, in Parliament and abroad. I had done some of the work of Moses Montefiore, travelling across Eastern Europe – Romania, Hungary, Czechoslovakia – crying 'Let my people go'. The Soviets blocked my way into Russia, but I laboured from without, pursued by the spectres of my murdered relatives.

During the debate on the War Crimes Bill, I described to a crowded Commons the tragedy of the murder of my relatives. A viciously right-wing Conservative who later met his ignoble and well-deserved political death, commented aloud: 'They burned the wrong half'.

I had become Enemy Number One of the British Fascists, and a favourite target of anti-Zionists and of Soviet Communists alike.

We gathered over time a band of British Jewish brothers, of like mind and purpose. Together with that great bridge-builder, the late Rabbi Hugo Gryn, and with Dr Richard Stone, a man deeply and tirelessly committed to peace and understanding, we started a Foundation, in the name of Maimonides. Led by that respected scholar and philanthropist, Dr David Khalili, we started creating a relationship between people who knew each other too little and from too far – Jews and Muslims, in Britain and overseas.

At first, we met suspicion and concern at almost every turn. From both sides. Now we are making progress. Now people are beginning to realize that while we needed these personal and quiet contacts in good times, that need is redoubled when relations are rough.

The decision is made. Sakhnin, here I come. Hired car . . . hired portable phone . . . copies of all the Arabic tapes that Douglas had ever made for me . . . 'Good luck' and 'take care' and an occasional 'rather you than me' from well-wishers. And away, back to my youth.

To Israel, yes. But not to the Israel I had known. Instead, to recognize a compounded irony – I know the Jewish population so well and its Arabs not at all. Arab and Jewish Israelis share the same land, live in the same land but occupy separate enclaves. Maybe I will find and open a door between them.

Chapter Two

JERUSALEM TO SAKHNIN

7.15 – Children's voices – my grandchildren. I climb upstairs from my cosy basement grandpa room, in Laura and David's suburban Jerusalem home. Natan, aged three, is standing in his black shorts, beaming. 'I'm having breakfast. Are you having breakfast?'

I stagger up to wish good morning to granddaughter Tali, aged five. She bestows on me another of my favourite beaming smiles. Then I slump back to bed for another half-hour's sleep.

8.30 – Laura: 'Where are you?' I had travelled to Israel by the Friday night, almost sleepless and by a very uncomfortable British Airways flight, where it makes about three inches of difference if you fly Club. 'The car won't be ready till 11.00,' said Laura. David has taken Tali off to kindergarten. Maybe Laura and I will have time for a swim.

I phoned the car hire company, whose name should be obliterated from the world of commerce. They told me that my original car had been booked for 11.00, but that I could have an Astra at 10.30. 'Fine,' I said.

Many huge smiles from Ella Avigail, born on 17 January. I saw her arrive – one of the greatest privileges of my life. Just three weeks after Myra had died – after the worst and longest years and weeks and days of my life. When the baby smiles, she looks like Myra. Myra chose the name Avigail, which means: Joy of my father – both fathers, David and me.

Laura takes me to the hire company and waits to make sure that I am all right. The man in charge turns out to be without question the slowest and most irritating human being in the world of car hire. His mind, his words and his actions are all in bottom gear.

My host in Sakhnin, Abdullah, phones. He tells me that the journey will take me three hours. He will wait for me at 2.00 p.m. in the only petrol station in town. He wishes me a safe journey. Most of this in Arabic, which pleases me. But time is dragging on.

Eventually, the car arrives. I presume that the printed hire form contains the usual term, stating that I have received the vehicle in good order. 'It's fine,' the manager says. 'Excellent . . . a new car . . . no problem . . .'

I notice that the ashtray does not retract. Not important, but I point it out to the man and ask if there is anything else wrong. 'Yes,' he says. 'Come outside and I'll show you.' The casing for the nearside wing mirror is missing. 'Not important,' he says.

He shows me how everything operates and off I go. Then I notice a yellow light glowing on the windscreen and drive the car round the block and back. 'What's that?' I ask. 'Not important,' he says. 'It will go off. It goes off and on.'

'So what is it?'

'You'll need to fill up with petrol.'

'Oh, isn't it full?'

'No. In this country, it doesn't have to be.'

Well, fancy that. Never mind. I'll fill up on the way. So off I go again. Then I notice that the air-conditioning is not working properly – and nor is the tape machine. Krikler's voice is crackling.

That doesn't matter much, but the air-conditioning does. Laura has insisted that I carry bottles of water, in case the car breaks down. I am sweating profusely, and the well-known Greville Janner cool has evaporated totally. Back again.

The manager laughs. 'Please don't get excited,' he says, lifting his right hand with the thumb and forefingers clasped together, in the way that I hate most because it combines discourtesy with disrespect. It has the Middle Eastern eloquence of the Western two-fingered V sign. 'No problem. Not important.'

I tell him in my best Hebrew that there is indeed a huge problem. The air-conditioning does not work properly.

'Have the car for the week for 400 dollars instead of 500 dollars,' he says.

'No!' I shout at him, in both Hebrew and English. 'No air-conditioning, no car.' He is still laughing.

'Get me another car!' I yell.

'You can have one at half past two,' he says.

To avoid a heart attack, I take a deep breath. I say very quietly: 'No – now!'

'The boss is coming,' he says. 'Here he is.'

The boss speaks English with an American accent. He does not say 'sorry' but offers me an American car, a Cavalier, which will cost me (he says) an extra 50 dollars for the week. To hell with that – let's have it. I point out that the air-conditioning in the wreck is not working.

'It's not defective,' he says. 'Just not working as well as it should.'

No point in arguing. The Cavalier is fine. Automatic shift, too. But by then I am in such a stew that I cannot find my black bag – ah yes, it is in my hand!

I ask the boss whether this car has a full tank of petrol and he says: 'No. But in this country, you bring the car back with the same amount of petrol in it that it had when you got it and we make a note and no problem.'

So I drive off and stop at the petrol station near to the King David Hotel – and that's where my happiness begins. No self-service, which is just as well, because I cannot get the petrol cap open or the alarm off. The two attendants are beaming. We talk Arabic and I manage to make myself understood and they congratulate me and we are all happy.

Oil? Only half full. But the water level is fine – thank God for that. *Ya Salaam!* – brilliant! And Dougie's voice emerges from the tape recorder, uncrackled Krikler, and I am off – on my favourite road in the world, the highway from Jerusalem to the Dead Sea.

Through the white, pink, brown hills and haze and sands of the desert. Past Bedouin encampments. Past that permanent, statuesque, hobbled camel, available for photographs, by the sign that says SEA LEVEL. And down to the lowest spot on the world's surface. Thank God for the operative air-conditioning.

I miss the bypass for Tiberias and stop at one of the world's lowest restaurants, for some *shoko* – chocolate milk, from the desert kibbutz of Yotvata. Delicious. Then back up to the bypass.

I still wonder at the green patches in the khaki, rocky desert, and at the extraordinary people who have created and maintained them. What a hell of a place to live.

The road up the Jordan Valley is largely deserted, as befits the desert. The problem (as Laura kept reminding me) is that people go much too fast and sometimes fall asleep at the wheel and 'You will drive carefully, won't you Daddy?' You bet. *Bi ta'keed.* Certainly.

Up the Jordan valley, past startling slashes of tropical trees and plants, which brighten the lives and journeys of visitors and locals alike. Along, onto the dangerous curves, with the security fence to the right, the mountains of Jordan ahead and the desert to the left. The great heat, browning the grass and the scrub. Frequent comfort stops – Laura has filled my mind with fears of dehydration so I have filled my stomach with bottled water. Up, up through the Valley, to the blue Sea of Galilee, glistening in a hollow of the brown, sandy mountains.

Police cars clustered around a broken crash barrier on a bridge – a car has gone over the edge. Its passengers are probably in hospital or dead. Janner, drive carefully. Keep to the right. Why *do* these foreigners insist on driving on the wrong side of the road? It's *davka* – just to spite us.

Watch towers, looking out across the green patches of plantations, on the far side of the Jordan. No rush – drive slowly, still, soak it in and enjoy. Time for Douglas's tapes.

When I used to drive with Myra, we'd get into the car and switch on the motor and Douglas's voice would emerge from the tape recorder. 'Oh, not Dougie . . .' she would say, shaking her head. She loved Dougie, but not his voice in the car teaching me Arabic. Well, it's my Arabic week – so, 'I love playing backgammon but I'm not very good at it . . . Is it your turn or mine?' Or: 'I am a magician – watch, I'll make this coin vanish . . . *Hawi samawi* . . .' – the open road and a new tape to learn.

Through Beth Shaan. I first visited the place in 1950, with my sister, Ruth. It had taken us seven days to reach Israel. Ferry to Paris. Train to Le Havre. Zim Line, the good ship *Kedma*, to Israel – first view, Mount Carmel. In many ways, you could condition yourself much better for change, when it took a week to arrive.

Now it's a desert town with white apartment blocks and red-roofed houses and neat roads and a stopping point en route to Tiberias, with views, as always, across to Jordan.

It was in Beth Shaan that I saw and little understood Bernard Shaw's *Pygmalion*, in Hebrew, one evening in the town's great open-air amphitheatre. It was packed with kibbutzniks, many of them with rifles slung over their shoulders.

I pass a signpost to Tirat Zvi – an orthodox kibbutz. There, where my old friend, Alfie Sherwood – a colleague from my days as a war crimes investigator in Germany – had settled himself into the agricultural life of the communal farm.

Past a neat, white graveyard. Myra, I miss you.

Past the sign, 'Scenic route to Gilboa'. Gan Ner – the village named after my parents – is in the Gilboa foothills. I'll be back there on Thursday, for the opening ceremony of their new leisure area. And then I'll go over the extraordinary tale of how the name 'Janner' metamorphosed into 'Gan Ner' and in the process not only translated into a garden of light but into homes for hundreds.

Past a sign to Haifa. Another to Afula. In 1950, near here, I had learned Hebrew – staying in children's villages and houses, with youngsters I had worked with when I was a sergeant in the War Crimes Group and they were in the Bergen Belsen Jewish Displaced Persons' Camp. In the *Kinderheim* – the children's home. Funny to think that they are now all grandparents, like me. Except for Boaz Karvy, Aharon Taler and Yosef Ilush, killed in wars and accidents, while serving in young Israel's Defence Forces. When I first knew them – in 1946, just after the end of the war – there was no Israel. No place on earth where these children were wanted.

In Sakhnin, there are no Jews. There is an invisible barrier between the Abrahamic tribes. Perhaps it is easier for people to live apart, but it is no way to share a country. You must treat racism against the other as an attack on yourself.

Strange how some proverbs cross the barriers of language. Like: '*Al aiman yazahzih al jebal*' – faith moves mountains. I found later Abdullah has faith in people. We should all learn from him and maybe we can shift some of those ranges of misunderstanding and of ignorance, which create those ranges of racist dislike.

It was the emergence of the Jewish State which provided a haven for people like the children in the Belsen Kinderheim – a state where they could live in peace and understanding not only with their neighbours but also and especially with the Arabs in their midst.

All of which (I thought) led me to Sakhnin, and to at least some reasonable use of the Arab language, if only to make people smile at my clumsy tongue.

I drive past kibbutzim that had split up – cracked apart on the anvil of internal early Israel politics, under the pressures of the Left, so long ago. Along the shores of the Sea of Galilee, with its beaches and tourists, and its fresh-fish-eating places, umbrellas with straw hats and tourists lounging, lying and sleeping with no shirts, in blazing heat. Lunatics. Swimmers in the lake and palm trees by the hillside and flaring, mauve and scarlet bushes and trees with blazing orange.

My mobile phone rings. I pull in. It's Laura. 'Where are you? How are you?' I was happy to tell her that I cannot remember when I had last enjoyed a journey like this.

There's white Tiberias now, on the hillside. I'm driving around the lake. Christ walked on these waters.

Past the fabled horns of Hittim. Here's where Saladin defeated the Crusaders.

I first came across the Horns of Hittim in the late James Michener's great book, *The Source*. From the road at least, it's a funny-looking hillock, with bits sticking out each end.

I'm getting more excited, as I turn onto Route 65, up over the hills of the north. The border with Lebanon is only about 50 miles away. Ever greener, with scrubland covering the mountainsides.

Now the turn off for Eilabun. Arab territory. The landscape, the buildings, Arabic language on shop signs. My last chance to turn back.

Some friends had warned me against being alone in an Arab town. As a notorious Zionist, would I be safe? I reckoned that I was in greater danger on the road to Sakhnin than I would be when I arrived. Anyway, I'm going. *Khalas* – what the hell!

Past some fine new stone houses alongside the road, flanked by electricity pylons. the road needs resurfacing – badly. Cows coming straight at me. Keep to the right. No need for the 60 km an hour speed limits signs here. Thirty is fine.

The road curls through the hills. Am I lost?

I stop at a bus station and call out to some men in working clothes, waiting for buses I supposed. In my best Arabic: 'Where's Sakhnin, please?'

'Down to the cross roads and turn left,' they reply – in Hebrew. '*Shukran*' – thank you. I hoot to them and wave as I go by and they wave back. I'm happy. Another friendly encounter. Why am I expecting anything else? Because until now, they are strangers.

Arab strangers, whom I don't know. Someone described antisemitism as 'dislike of the unlike'. I wonder how unlike I will find my Arab hosts and whether I will meet dislike, as a Jewish stranger. So far, so good.

Down into another valley. A dead dog, drying out beside the road and fabulous views across the valley to the mountains and villages to the north. Won't be long now.

A car with an idiot driver passes a lorry and roars up to my exhaust pipe. I pull over to let him by and he flashes his lights and waves his thanks. As my mother used to say: 'He's in a hurry to die.' It was my pleasure to postpone that evil day.

I turn left towards the Arab town of Dir Hanna. A fine, wide road. Crash barrier to the right, so that I don't swerve off down the mountainside. Plenty of new building work. Sakhnin is somewhere to the right but there's no sign. Except – 'Petrol station, 600 metres.' Let's ask the way. There's a hotel next door, with signs in Hebrew and in Arabic.

I ask the garage attendant, in my best Arabic: 'Where's Sakhnin, please?' He replies in English. 'About eight kilometres.' Five miles. Next junction. A sign, at last, 'Sakhnin, 4 kilometres'. Hooray!

A lad hitch-hiking. If the car was cleaner, I'd give him a lift. But the front seat is cluttered with water bottles, dictating machines, portable telephone, Walkman and earphones.

Ahead to the right is a minaret, at the top of the hill. Sakhnin!

I'm to meet Abdullah in the only petrol station in town. Now, what the hell is 'petrol station' in Arabic? I used to know.

Hebrew signs advertising Levi jeans and El Al Flights, Sakhnin Tours and Agfa films. Other signs in both Hebrew and Arabic. I've remembered, petrol station is *Mahatat Benzin*.

Two minarets now. But where's the *Mahatat Benzin*? Past an Arab in a red and white *kafieh* head-dress, driving a crawling tractor.

I phone Abdullah on my mobile and try to explain to him in three languages that I'm in town but can't find the petrol station. 'I'm outside the Discount Bank.'

'I'll come for you,' he says. 'What colour is your car?'

'White,' I reply.

Three minutes later, there's Abdullah, also in a white car. We lower our windows and smile. I say, in Douglas's poshest Arabic: '*Asalamu Aleikum Warahmat Ulla Wa Barakutu.*' He replies: '*Asalumu Aleikum – Marhaban* – welcome. Follow me!'

I am so excited that I forget to start the car before I put it into drive. A truck hoots. We're off. Winding our way through the narrow streets. Arab music pouring out of a café. Round a corner and down a hideously steep, narrow alley, with walls each side, and whitewashed, concrete houses. Pull up outside one of them on its thick concrete stilts. Opposite is a sign: SHADI GUEST HOUSE. I've arrived.

Chapter Three

THE SHADI GUEST HOUSE

'This is your home,' says Abdullah Halayle. 'You are in my family. This is my wife, Fawzieh.' She is tall, dark-haired and smiling. '*Merhaban*,' she says, 'Welcome'.

They have four children, two boys – Jowdat, aged thirteen, and Shadi, eight – the guest house is named after him. Two girls – Jihen, eleven, and Asmahan, ten. 'They are your family,' says Abdullah.

The dining and living room is small and narrow – maybe fifteen feet by ten. A phone in one corner, refrigerator in another. Table and chairs in the middle. In troop the children, smiling, ear to ear. My new family.

Do I drink tea? Tea with mint? Certainly, *minfadlak* – please.

All in Arabic. I was pleased with myself. Douglas would be proud. I could make myself understood, *alhamdulillah* – God be praised.

We sat on the green lawn at the end of the patio, on a rubber mattress, with gaily coloured cushions. The next hour and a half

28

was a mixture of magic, laughter and lessons.

Jowdat was learning English and he produced his book. We went through the letters, translating from A to Z – from Ape to Zebra, in English – my job – and then into Arabic – theirs. Huge laughter as I mispronounced those horrendous gutturals that make Arabic such a problem for the uninitiated.

Then Mr Shaaban Saleh telephoned. He was going to be my teacher. 'There's a wedding on this evening. Would you like me to take you to it?' And how.

But we did not wait for him to arrive because as dusk swooped down on us, the sounds of the wedding echoed along the hilly alley. We walked up it, Abdullah and I. It was the men-only, day-before-the-wedding, open-air gathering. Two singers were chanting into hand-held microphones, in melodic monotone. I sat beside the head teacher of the High School, who spoke English and explained what was happening. The singers, he said, were welcoming the guests. Now they were welcoming me. People came by and shook my hand. '*Merhaban . . .*' '*Merhabtayn*' – a double welcome to you, I replied. Everyone was smiling at me.

Then the politics began and they told me in the most friendly and matter-of-fact way that they considered that for 50 years they had endured discrimination. Lands on the outskirts of the town had been confiscated, so they were limited in the area in which they could build. Yes, there was still land for building but it took away from their fields. Half the men worked outside the town – in Karmiel, Haifa, Afula and other places. Unemployment, though, is not more than ten per cent.

A man told me that he was a computer expert and had applied for a job with the Israel National Electric Company but was turned down because he was an Arab. 'They think we're enemies,' he said. 'They say that we are security risks.' I was shocked. That was racism. Totally unacceptable. They used the excuse that he had not served in the Israel Defence Forces. But Arabs – other than Druze – are not accepted by the Israeli armed forces.

★

I have always hated any form of discrimination. Whether against Arabs or Jews, Asians or Blacks, women or gays or anyone else in a decent minority, it is to me inexplicable, inexcusable and revolting.

It may be direct and open, like the Nazi: 'Alle Juden raus' – Jews, get out. Or disguised, but totally obvious, such as 'All applicants must have served in the Israel Defence Forces' – which excludes Arabs (but not, incidentally, Druze). Or it may be more subtle like Britain's former and now happily banned discrimination against women, by refusing employment protection rights to part-timers, over 90 per cent of whom are female.

Much of my work in this field was with Leicester's Asian community.

There was once a large factory near to the Belgrave Road, itself a largely Asian residential area. On a parliamentary visit, I noticed that there were no Asian employees. I asked the management why this was and they said: 'We don't know. We certainly don't ban Asians.'

I asked whether there was indirect discrimination. In my experience, barristers' clerks, for instance, and Covent Garden porters used to pass on their jobs to members of their own family. 'No, not with us. But we'll look into it.'

They did. Guess what they found? An Asian would come to the factory gate and say to the gatekeeper: 'I've come to apply for the job, advertised in the *Leicester Mercury*.' The gatekeeper would reply: 'I'm terribly sorry, sir, but the job is gone.' Result: no Asian employees! The gatekeeper was soon on his way out and Asian employees on their way in.

It was in the Working Men's Clubs that I used to run into the most open racist bias. Not against me as a Jew. Anti-Jewish bias was never the least problem for me, in the good city of Leicester. No, it was: 'Why do you only look after *them*?' I knew who 'them' was, of course.

'I look after everyone,' I would reply. 'I am your MP and will look after you. I am their MP and I will care for them. I don't make any distinctions because of people's colour or race or origin

– and nor, my friend, should you.' Then I would move on, leaving my constituent shaking his or her head in profound disagreement.

Worse: 'When are you going to get rid of *them*?' Or they would use an epithet which I will not dignify by putting into print, but which is the Asian equivalent of 'Yids'. At which stage I would blaze up in anger and walk off. Sometimes they would shout after me: 'We're not going to vote for you again.'

I'd come back and say: 'That's your decision, friend. If you get rid of me, I hope you'll get someone who'll look after the people round here as well as I do. Good luck.'

Anyway, my attacker would probably vote for the National Front or not at all. Racism is a filthy disease.

We have done well in Leicester. The answer to racism is to stand up to it.

The race relations world has invented a new watch-word: diversity. How boring life would be if we were all the same. No danger of that: but you have to live with diversity and cope with it. Respect the diversity of others as you would have them respect yours. Celebrate our differences in harmony together.

Israel should join the Commonwealth, which teetered on the edge of extinction in the sad days of South African apartheid. Separate but unequal.

Some of Israel's enemies try to draw comparisons between South Africa before freedom and the Jewish State now. Which is total rubbish. Ask at the Shadi Guest House and they will tell you. But both Arabs and Jews have much to learn from Nelson Mandela.

Myra and I visited the great man, in his African National Congress headquarters, soon after his release from jail and detention. With her customary bluntness, Myra asked him: 'How can you deal with these people, who kept you locked up in Robben Island for 29 years'.

'My dear lady,' he replied. 'In this life, you must look to the future. You cannot build a good future on the tortures of the past.'

It is pointless for Israel's Arabs to say: 'We once owned that land . . .' Or: 'That land belonged to our town. It was stolen from us, 50 years ago.'

Yes, you have to look back at the past, to mould the future. In South Africa, to ensure freedom for all races. In Israel, equality for all peoples. For us Jews, who found our inspiration through seeking a return to the land which we left not 50 but 2000 years ago, to recognize the longings of Arabs in their Diaspora, with their ancestral memories and their legitimate, national aspirations.

Like Mandela, we must all look to the future. *Hayk adunya* – that's fate. That's life. The alternative is, at best, more strife, more ill-will. At worst, death. Racism is the precursor, the forerunner, the first diseased step towards the death of decency.

Racism may be individual or state. Nazi Germany, Austria, Vichy France . . . On occasion, post-war Poland – only a few thousand Jews left there, but I remember when one of their post-war governments blamed 'the Jews' for their nasty famine.

Then there was Switzerland. It was at their specific request that the German Nazis stamped the letter 'J' on the passports of Jews, so that the Swiss could know whom to exclude. Yet the enrichment of their nation through business with the Nazis was generally motivated, I believe, through financial cupidity, not racist hatred. They certainly accepted gold from the Nazis which had been melted down from the jewellery and even the teeth of concentration camp victims. But they took far more from the looted treasuries of Nazi-occupied lands.

When the pressure to make at least some reasonable restitution got too hot for them, their then President denounced Jews for 'blackmail' and their Ambassador to the United Nations said that the time had come 'to declare war' on the World Jewish Congress.

Happily, the Swiss Government and its new President reacted vigorously to this racist rubbish. Then the Swiss banks established their Humanitarian Fund, and later paid huge sums for restitution.

Still, Swiss antisemites have scuttled out from under their alpine rocks. Too many have accused my colleagues and myself of 'creating antisemitism'.

Those who attack racism of any sort do not create racism – racists do that.

There are even Jewish people who say: 'Hush. Do not stir up trouble. Do not talk about restitution and money – that creates antisemitism.'

My reply is always the same. 'Have you learned nothing? Do you not know that unless we fight for our Jewish people, then we have no right to ask or expect anyone else to do so for us. Hold your head up!'

One other ingredient is immediate action. Do not wait. Attack the disease before it spreads.

Ogden Nash wrote: 'The trouble with a kitten is that/Eventually it becomes a cat!' Racists are rats. Do not let them grow fat on your silence.

In the words of Rabbi Hillel: 'If I am not for myself, who will be for me?' He continued: 'But if I am only for myself, what am I?' We must do battle against racism directed against any other human being. And get on with it, while life lasts. 'If not now, then when?'

The principal motivations in my political life have been deep hatred of poverty and of discrimination. Acceptance of my father's honourable principle: 'We British Jews,' he told me, 'we are privileged to live in a decent land and we are morally obliged to give service to its people. But on the basis that we do a much better job for Britain by retaining our Jewish pride and roots than we would if we tried to hide them.' That included the duty to campaign for the creation of a Jewish state – as my father did with unremitting courage, when Zionism was deeply unpopular. And then to work for its democratic stability and its acceptance into the world community.

I always admired my father's immense courage. He campaigned constantly for his constituents, without regard to their religion or race. He often spoke alone in Parliament, on behalf of the Jewish people. He also taught me that if we do stand tall, sensibly and with dignity, and demand our Jewish rights, we will have many allies. In his day, it was Josiah (Lord) Wedgwood, the magnate of the potteries, and other colleagues on the Parliamentary Anglo-Palestine Group. For me, today, it is a host of well-loved non-Jewish allies, of many political parties and religions. Without them, we Jews have no hope. With them, we are strong.

Racism, in any form, is loathsome. The question in each case is: how best to react.

I first stood for Parliament in 1955. I was Labour candidate for Wimbledon, a seat with a Tory majority of over 18,000. It was fun. Parliamentary elections always are, when you know either that you cannot win or that you cannot lose. At that time Wimbledon was unwinnable for Labour.

Jack Gibson was my agent – an official of the Union of Shop Distributors and Workers, in his mid-sixties. A fighter, whom Myra and I both loved. Such hair as he had left was white, swept back along the sides of his pink and naked scalp. He was charming, shrewd and outspoken.

One day, Jack cycled up to our committee room, beaming. He came in, rubbing the knuckles of his right hand, joyful from ear to ear.

'Why are you so happy, Jack?' Myra asked him.

'Well, my dear, I've just won an argument,' he said. 'Somebody asked me how I could be the agent for a bloody Jew. I hit him on the nose!'

A great answer, but not always appropriate. Especially from a size-challenged person like myself.

To reason with a racist – a real racist, that is – is hopeless. But sometimes people make racist remarks because they are ignorant or afraid. I learned this in 1970, when I received a letter from a constituent, who was out of work and in great need, complaining that 'they' – Asians, whom he described in foul racist language – were taking Leicester people's jobs and homes and 'living off the Social' and getting more money than he was.

34

I decided to see the man and to listen to him. He and his family lived in poverty of every kind, financial and educational. I accessed help for them, which they did not know was available. Then, on a second visit, I explained to them that our new Asian community was not taking resources from our city, but putting them in – creating more employment than they used. Family people, interested in educating their children. People who looked after their old in a way that we should be doing but do not.

'You're right,' he said. 'I'm sorry.'

I receive much fascist, racist and antisemitic mail. My staff send it on to the appropriate people to look it over – which include the police, when it contains threats. But they give me those letters whose writers might learn through explanation. I write back to them saying: 'As I would like to think that you did not intend your letter to be personally offensive, I am replying to you with courtesy.' I then answer the points made. Nearly every time, I receive a letter of apology.

I fought for anti-racist legislation. Its opponents said: 'You are interfering with freedom of speech. Laws cannot change attitudes.' Wrong. They can, they do and they will alter people's approach to diversity. And we already interfere with freedom of speech – through laws and against (for example) pornography or libel.

Law and education must be partners in the constant fight for people to respect the rights of others. That is pontificating. Action is what we need. Plus priority.

In the early 1970s, the common belief – which I neither shared nor, I regret, openly opposed – was that if you publicly slammed the National Front or other neo-fascist, right-wing and racist political organizations, they would savour the breath of publicity and we would transform small, insignificant and largely unknown groups into popular advocates for the deprived and disadvantaged.

In 1974, two of their candidates came within about 50 votes of winning seats on the Leicester City Council. They did so on a racist, anti-Asian and anti-immigrant platform, in an area of my constituency where almost no immigrants, Asian or black, had

35

their homes.

We decided to change tack. When the next elections arrived, we put into every letter-box a pamphlet with the headline: 'The National Front is a Nazi Front'. Their vote collapsed when people knew the truth. The vast majority of British people hate Nazis. They or their fathers or grandfathers fought against Hitler. But it was no solution for us to sit back and hope that racism would quietly fade away.

Still, no Asians at that time entered the doors of Working Men's Clubs. Afro-Caribbeans were usually welcome. Why? Because blacks were few; Asians were more numerous and their community was growing fast. People regarded them as a threat. It is not just dislike of the unlike and of the unknown. It is fear.

Yes, it is not that different in Israel. Jews fear Arabs and too many believe the stereotypes of 'Muslim extremists' and 'terrorists'. Conversely, too many Arab citizens fear 'the Jews'.

God bless Abdullah and the Shadi Guest House. I wonder if there are any guest houses in Jewish Israel, who seek an Arab clientele and get it – and look after them, like the Halayles looked after me.

In Israel, of course, they have proportional representation. So there are no constituency MPs. No one whose job it is to care specifically and all the time for the people of Sakhnin, and whom they can get rid of if they don't like. My constituents were fully entitled to say: 'If you are not going to work to repatriate the Asians, we are not going to vote for you.' Equally, I was proud to look after everyone, not least my Asian community, and to hang on to what was during those 27 years a marginal seat.

Israel should have a constituency system. Then the people of Sakhnin would have their own voice in the Knesset – the Israeli Arabs' Parliament, as much as it is the Parliament of Israel's Jewish citizens.

Meanwhile, we need education, national and international. Its basis: that racism in your community against any other is your problem. Conversely: racism in other people's communities against yours is their problem.

I remembered that a few years ago, the Reverend Al Sharpton, whom the American Jewish community regarded as an antisemitic rabble-rouser – was due to visit England. I arranged a meeting with a black lawyer friend, a respected leader of Britain's Afro-Caribbean community. He said to me: 'What do you want me to do about it?'

I replied: 'If there's any sort of actual or incipient black or other racist problem in my Jewish community, that's a problem for me. Sharpton's visit here is a problem for you. It's for you to handle.'

He agreed, and he did. The effects of the visit were greatly subdued and reduced as a result.

If this were Britain, I would refer all those complaining of discrimination to their local Members of Parliament. Under Israel's system of proportional representation, they do not have one. I am increasingly reinforced in my profound opposition to PR. In theory, it is fairer. In practice, it robs individuals and their families, intimate and extended, and their towns and cities, their racial minorities and their special interests, of the individual representation which they need and deserve. Which includes the right to remove those representatives who do not, in their view, represent their interests in their Parliament. And those interests certainly include the right not to be discriminated against on grounds of race, colour, nationality or ethnic origins. In today's Sakhnin, they have no MP to represent them.

We were joined by a squat, bald, serious man, in a blue suit and open-necked shirt. He had been mayor of the town for many years and was now retired but working for the Democratic Front Party. The headmaster and he agreed that there were no facilities for young people – no swimming pool in the town, with its 20,000 people. They had been starved of resources by successive governments and had just ended a strike. They could not even pay the wages of the civil servants. They had overspent their municipal budget, because it was too small.

Yes, this was the place where, in 1976, there had been land riots and people killed and there's a memorial to them. Look, there's a Jewish village on the mountain opposite, with red roofs and a valley in between. No, there's little contact between the people in the two towns. The headmaster told me that if he drove there with his car, people would wonder what he was about.

A bunch of youngsters shook my hand and smiled and listened to the complaints. One of them said: 'Well, it all goes back to the British Empire, doesn't it?'

'What a marvellous thought,' I exclaimed. 'Blame the British!' Fifty years later . . . 'Well, we've got a new government in Britain now and there's no point in blaming them. And Israel sometimes elects the wrong people, just like we did for 18 years.' They laughed. Curiously, I think they meant it. It's the legacy of the British Empire, isn't it? Divide the citizens and rule.

Too many of Britain's leaders of the time were anti-Zionist, from gut to brain, from thought to action. And Britain did the Jews of Palestine no avoidable favours.

Equally, Israel's Jews had much to resent. There was the infamous *Exodus*, for instance – the ship with its load of Jewish survivors of the Holocaust, turned back from Israel and returned to Europe. Not to Cyprus. Not to Mauritius. But (of all places) to Germany.

British soldiers decanted the refugees into internment camps in northern Germany, in Wilhelmshaven and Am Stau.

I thought of my visits to these camps, my loathing of Bevin's policies and my identification with the miseries of the refugees and my anger and anguish. I did not visit the *Exodus* camps in my army uniform. Even in civilian clothes, I felt guilty.

When I first visited Israel, just two years after its birth, I expected to feel guilty – to meet anti-British hatred, open or more subtle. To my surprise and pleasure, I found very little. Instead, Britain was the model. Parliament, police and Civil Service, courts, law and above all, incorruptible justice – all on much and openly admired British models. The Hebrew language had absorbed British words, some of them very curious – like 'kvacker', for porridge – Quaker Oats. My favourite: the back axle of a car was its 'beckex'. Its front axle: 'the beckex kidmi' – the back axle of the front.

What, then, of 'divide and rule'? British administrators did not have to divide Arab from Jew. History and reality did that for them. But certainly they did nothing to bind the communities, and they left Palestine at war – a war which they were confident that the tiny Jewish *yishuv* – a settlement of some 600,000 people, in a vast Arab world – was bound to lose. Lucky they were wrong, I thought.

The droning singing of the dancers tugged me back to reality. The men formed themselves into a traditional, pulsating oval, slowly stepping round to the same throbbing, musical monotony, filling the junction of four roads with their rhythmic swaying.

I sat with the school teacher and the ex-mayor and we watched. Then I slipped back home, to phone Laura and David, and to set their minds at rest. Dad was fine. *Mumtaz* – splendid.

Then back to the wedding, and my present to the groom. Most people, I was told, give between 100 and 1000 shekels – about £20 to £200. I gave him a House of Commons pill-box. I still have access to the souvenir shop, so there is something left of my parliamentary glory. He was pleased. He pushed it into his back pocket, thanked me, shook hands, and danced on, in the centre of the elongated ring of smiling men.

Home again, and Abdullah insisted that I dine with him. Fabulous fish, with salads and pitta bread and soft drinks, served by Fawzieh. Hospitality at its height. We ate on our own, in the cool of the patio. Abdullah tried to practise his English on me and I begged him to be patient and let me learn my Arabic from him. One way and another, we chatted about the wedding and the guests, but neither he nor I ever talked politics together.

A neighbour called Jamal – a member of Abdullah's extended family, the *hamoula* – came by and offered me Arabic lessons. 'I

39

don't want anything from you,' he said. 'Only please regard it as part of our pleasure that you have come to visit us.' I thanked him and promised to be in touch. He is a man of about 30, solid and tanned.

11.15, *mabsoot* – contented – but disturbed that after 50 years, these folk are still not integrated into Israel's Jewish society. The best way to turn them into enemies is to treat them as enemies. I have new friends.

Where have I been, these 50 years? Always in touch with Israel, but never sensitive to the two societies.

Why is this? Partly because I have been wearing Jewish blinkers. I looked in the direction of the suffering and the hardship, the trials and the triumphs, of the Jewish State and of those survivors, especially the ones whom I knew and of whom I was fond. My family lived and lives in the Jewish bubble.

Israeli Jewish politicians move out into the Arab world to keep their electoral links, to win votes and to seek support. Or, if you are a cynic, to avoid trouble, batten down hatches and keep the Arab population at least sufficiently content to avoid an internal fifth column.

Foreign politicians, like myself, concentrate on the overall Palestinian-Israeli or Arab world problems. We overlook, literally as well as metaphorically, Israel's Arab citizens.

Equally, they are on the whole satisfied to stay apart. They may come into Jewish cities, towns or villages, to work or even to shop. But they live apart – their social life, almost wholly – their business life, largely – their political lives, to a surprising extent. Two peoples apart, in a land they share. We must build bridges.

I lie back on my firm and comfortable bed, more than content with my first day in this Israel Arab world. The air-conditioning is on and the room cool. Beside my bed are some foil-wrapped blue chocolates, with the word 'Spira' on them.

My mobile phone rings. It is David, from Jerusalem, just checking that I am in good shape. I tell him that everything is *bekhair* – fine. But on a whim, I ask him about the unusual Spira chocolates.

'Don't eat them!' he cries. 'They are mosquito repellent pads! They go into a container which plugs into the wall and it poisons the flying beasts. If you eat them they will poison you!'

I have come here to learn . . . and this morsel of learning arrived just in time.

Chapter Four

SAKHNIN

I am happy here not to be recognized. Yes, they know that I am a stranger in town. They guess that I am Jewish and they check it out by greeting me with warm Shaloms. But I enjoy the freedom of the personally unrecognized.

It is not the same in Jerusalem. Not long ago, I was driving a car along a main road and I missed the turn-off. I put out my arm, waved, signalled and pulled gingerly across. A car drew up alongside me, lowered its window and the occupant called out: 'Mr Janner. It may be all right to drive like that in Hampstead Garden Suburb, but it won't do here in Jerusalem!' Oy vay!

Here in Sakhnin, I am the anonymous stranger. I hope they would greet and treat me as kindly if they knew of my Labour Zionist pedigree.

Then along comes Abdullah and introduces me as a British Member of Parliament and it is no good my saying, *sabeq – former* MP. He is determined that my former respect should still be accorded, so what the hell. After 27 years, I suppose it's OK, especially in Sakhnin.

Abdullah embellishes the introduction with a few words about my father's friendship with Moshe Sharett. I had unwisely showed him Sharett's picture on the 20 shekel piece.

This morning, I started work with my new teacher. Not the one who had phoned, but Jowdat, the chubby 13-year old. We sat on opposite sides of the table and he taught me basic Arabic and laughed, and I taught him basic magic and laughed. I learned new words and mispronounced them and we both laughed. He learned the mystic arts of palming and lapping and was not nearly as clumsy in magic as I am in Arabic, but we still laughed. And that was my hour's lesson in the morning. Much better than sitting with a formal teacher.

Magic is the world's greatest ice breaker. Especially for children, though children are harder to fool than adults, and adults enjoy the illusions of childhood.

When my son, Daniel, was President of the Cambridge Union, he met US President Richard Nixon for breakfast. Nixon told him that no politician needs more than half a dozen speeches. You simply adapt them.

As with speeches, so with magic. If you have half a dozen tricks or sleights or illusions which you perform really well, you can adapt them to audience and occasion.

If sleight of mind is the key to success in politics, so you need sleight of hand, for close-up magic. Once you can (for instance) produce or vanish coins, you can achieve precisely the same effect with stones from the path, crumbs from the table or brightly coloured bouncy balls from your pocket. That's where I start. And that's what won me attention, acceptance and laughter from my Arab hosts.

They all watched entranced as I produced balls from inside my empty hands and from behind their ears, from potted plants and from planted drawers. The children each chose some for themselves and bounced them away.

Watching my young hosts, I thought of my life-threatening moment, in a long career of magic. It was during my parliamentary visit to Arab Yemen.

My colleagues and I had sat around the walls in the vast *mafraj* – or receiving room – of Sheikh Abdullah bin Hussein Al Ahmar, ruler of the tribes of the north and our host. Around us were tribesmen, with white robes and curved daggers, and ministers and businessmen in smart Western suits.

Suddenly, two young children walked into the room and smiled shyly. 'The Sheikh's grandchildren,' my neighbour whispered. I signalled to one of the lads to come over to me. I produced a bouncy ball from behind his right ear and held out my right hand, inviting him to take the ball in his. When he found that my hand was empty, he screamed, *very* loudly. The room froze. Every tribesman's hand shot to his dagger. I stood, petrified – my end was nigh and magic was the cause of it.

I pulled the errant ball from my pocket, held it up, bowed and presented it to the lad. He did not move.

Then one of the men realized what had happened. '*Hooa Sahhar,*' he said. 'The man is a magician!' They all laughed, sheathed their daggers and I breathed again.

No such problem with my four young Sakhnini hosts. First day: entertainment. Second day: teach them one basic sleight. Third day: practice – and another, simple trick. Fourth day: just for Jowdat, the paddle trick – how to print both sides of a visiting card and then wipe them both off. In return, they shared with me the magic of their language.

Everyone loves magic. Adults are easier to deceive than children, but everyone enjoys seeing the impossible before their eyes.

I thought of that unforgettable occasion in Bucharest, shortly after the Romanians emerged from their Stalinist era. I led a group of MPs to see one of their horrendous orphanages. Never had I seen children so deprived, wretched, starved. It took just half a minute of magic to light up their sunken eyes and make them smile. Even for a moment.

Once my young Arab hosts knew that I was a magician, they told all their family, all the *hamoula*, and everyone else whom we met. I was a stranger no longer. The ice melted away with cries of 'Show us a trick!'

I blessed my magic mentors and friends and teachers – David Berglas, Paul Daniels, Cyril Golding, and other magicians, known and unknown, who had shared their art with me. Unlike Arabic or English, magic is the universal language of illusion, deception and misdirection. Just like politics, you might say. . .

Happily, it is holiday time, for children over 16. The junior school is still having classes but for some reason that I don't understand, Jowdat, who is only 13, is on holiday. His sisters and small brother spend their mornings at school.

Abdullah teaches chemistry in the senior school. He is free and has decided to look after me for the day. Off we went to the junior school – the only one in town. Some 1500 pupils, packed into a building constructed in the last days of the British mandate.

A happy school. Laughing, joyful, relaxed but respectful. Precisely the sort of atmosphere that I had learned to appreciate in some of the schools in my former Leicester West constituency, and the absence of which I regretted in some others.

The children were spotlessly clean – their faces and arms and hands and especially their clothes. And coolly, neatly dressed. It is, in a way, easier to dress well in very hot places like this because you wear less clothing. And it is certainly hot here. But I admired the parents who turned out these children so crisply. Like one little girl I noticed in a brightly coloured dress, with patent leather black shoes and socks with frills turned over the top of them. Children in neat, cool, short trousers or dresses. No school uniform, but every child scrubbed.

Only one girl was wearing a traditional Muslim head covering. They told me that in this village, the vast majority of people are secular. Not too many go to the mosque. But everybody draws a religious line at a different place. For instance, the head teacher whom I met last night at the outdoor wedding party will not go to the wedding party in the hall tonight because he does not drink alcohol and he does not want to be in a place where others do.

There is always drink in our Jewish weddings. We make blessings over wine, as we do over bread. But there is so little heavy drinking that caterers customarily charge more for Jewish gatherings than they do for others because they make so much less on the booze. Moderation in alcohol, if in little else.

The teacher also told me that this town is run by the secular. The Islamists are few and not strong and have nobody on the local council. Still, they may get one or two seats at the next election. They are not giving up. Yet in general Sakhnin is a modern place.

Not all the Arab towns are like this. Um al Fahm, for instance, and other towns which are nearer the border, are more affected by the West Bank. The nearer they come to the city of Jenin, the more likely they are to be extremist. Sakhnin is not. It is a pleasant place, like the school. The junior school has anything up to 40 in a class and the classrooms are not large. But the children are happy. When I come in, Abdullah introduces me to the teacher, who says, '*Ahlen – merhaban*' – Hello, welcome. The children rush up and shake my hand, their faces glowing.

I visit a class where they are teaching English to one of the upper grades. They know about as much English as our English youngsters of the same age know French, which is not much. They start with Arabic. Hebrew is their second language. English is the third. By then, they are out of linguistic breath.

Many of the children graduate to the high school, although some go out to work or on to craft or technical schools. There is compulsory schooling for all children – Arab or Jewish, of course – from the ages of five to sixteen.

We drive to the senior school where Abdullah teaches. The head's office has three portraits on the wall behind his desk. Yitzhak Rabin, with a black stripe across the right-hand corner. Ezer Weizmann, President of Israel. And a former head teacher. No Peres, no Netanyahu.

I wonder how Jewish schools compare. A picture of the President shows allegiance to the State, but is there always one of the current Prime Minister? I suspect that each head can do as he or she wishes. In my granddaughter Tali's kindergarten, there is a picture of the owner's favourite Indian guru.

I think of the Jewish school in Damascus. Like all other Syrian institutions, its ceiling was festooned with a barrage of pictures of President Assad, and of his son who was killed in a car accident.

We talk in English. 'There is no educational discrimination in Israel,' said the head. 'These children have the same chance of getting into Israeli universities as anyone else, but that is not a lot. It is very difficult. Many school graduates – Jewish and Arab – go to Czechoslovakia and Russia or anywhere else where they can get into college or university.'

On the wall to the right is a bookcase, with a row of bright, tawdry trophies crowding its top. On the other wall hangs a list of classes, with numbers and writing in Arabic and Hebrew. I asked him: Why Hebrew? 'For Jewish visitors,' he said.

The school is empty, but Abdullah proudly shows me the computer laboratory and his own chemistry rooms, in a sturdy, white building with windows open to the breezes.

Back to the head teacher, and another cup of sweet, black coffee. They live off it. Everywhere you go, you're offered a tiny cup of this tasty liquid. You take it and drink it. They offer you more and you shake the cup gently from side to side and you say: '*Shukran* – thank you, no more.'

These customs can be very important. Like the rule in Arab countries that if you sit, you do not point the soles of your feet at other people. You tuck your legs under you or put them flat along the ground.

Gestures, too, differ from culture to culture. I think of the amazing occasion when I enjoyed the Indian festival of Janmashtami – the celebration of the birth of the god Vishnu. A local band played on the rostrum in the town square. The drummer was brilliant and when I caught his eye, I did the thumbs-up signal for him. He collapsed with laughter and pointed me out to his friends and I gathered that in that area at least it was the equivalent of the two fingers V-sign in Britain!

The head is chain-smoking. I ask him whether that sets the right example to his youngsters and he says: 'My office is a smoking zone. It is not permitted anywhere else in the school.

'No, there is no real drug problem here – some hashish, but not much. And very little crime. Which is surprising, because there is nowhere for our students to enjoy their free time.'

If it is true that there is no drug problem, then the parents of Sakhnin are living in a blissful world, in which the words hash, crack and ecstasy retain their old fashioned, drugless meanings.

Not like London. Young friends tell me that 'jointless' parties scarcely exist, from teenage up. The problems spread across society. All praise to the *hamoula*, if its pleasures really do keep these miseries at bay. If the greatest worry for Abdullah and Fawzieh is the children's over-consumption of ice-cream, they are very lucky.

There is no swimming pool . . . no public gardens and few private ones . . . practically nowhere to play football except in the streets . . . no land for recreation . . . and no priority from the town council for recreation for the youngsters.

I asked him why recreational facilities have no priority. 'Surely, that's wrong?'

He shrugged. 'There are other priorities – the roads are very bad, for instance. And there's no money to pay salaries for teachers and civil servants, never mind for people to supervise recreation.'

What about some help for the school from the parents?

In both schools, they told me that there are parent-teachers' associations and parents do help, but marginally.

Happily, the community is very strong – the community and the extended families. The *hamoula* is each person's base. The family that lives around the Shadi Guest House, for instance. They are all related in some way and if you want to be regarded as a man or a woman of substance, then you must behave. Most people do.

I have learned much about the organization of the 'family' in other lands. In many African as well as Arab countries, tribes dominate. In Kuwait and Oman and other Gulf countries, royal families merge and rule – from the same tribe. I must find out more about the *hamoula*.

Back to the guest house for a sleep and to dictate my diary onto my tape recorder. My perennial poor planning: I did not bring enough tapes. I had not expected to write a book. So Abdullah drove me to a typical, small high street shop that sells music tapes and cosmetics, and men's toiletries. I bought blank tapes for my Walkman – a word which has now entered into the Arabic language. And some shaving cream.

At 2.30, after a sleep and some more recording, Abdullah, together with Jowdat and Shadi, took me to the local folk museum. The boys had never been there, and they weren't particularly excited at the prospect of seeing it.

Housed in an old Arab mansion, this is the most informal museum I have ever been in. The man in charge is a friend of David's – Amin Aburaye. He makes me very welcome. I notice a mobile phone on his belt. There are even more mobiles in Israel than in Hong Kong – or in London.

The courtyard is open and you walk around and handle the old agricultural implements. 'Here is the covered area where the animals were kept . . . Here are the tools the farmers used to cut the wheat . . .'

Inside, there's a *diwan* – a sitting room, which contrasted with the grand one in Kuwait, where one evening Douglas and I had met all the white-robed commercial and political giants and people came in and out and out and shook hands and talked and gossiped and drank sweet coffee. Or the *mafraj* – the room at the top of the Jewish house in the Yemen – in Sa'dah. During the day it was a sitting room, at night a dormitory, on the Sabbath their synagogue. And there they entertained us with glowing hospitality.

In the Sakhnin museum's *diwan* there were cushions around the wall with cloth models of village dignitaries, including the headman – the *Mukhtar* – and the priest – the *Imam* – and a guest

49

with a cloth cigar stuck in his mouth, which little Shadi enjoyed pulling out. We sat on the cushions between the models and treated them as if they were our friends. I noticed another model, sitting at the far end of the room, a singer with an antique and sadly silent lute.

Downstairs, there were exhibitions of ancient implements. 'Ancient' meant about 30 years old, and in some local villages they are still using them. A combination of lack of funds to modernize and the old traditions of subsistence farming on small plots, I suppose. In Jewish Israel, these implements vanished into museums, many years ago.

There were oil lanterns, which I recognized from my childhood cub camps. Scythes and tools, and a room full of costumes. Clothes for camels – they told me there was only one camel left in Sakhnin now, and he is in the courtyard of a restaurant, to be photographed with tourists.

A tour arrived. Teachers. One of them taught English and regaled me with stories about Big Ben and the Tower of London and why Big Ben was so named. He added: 'We must live in peace and respect each other, or we will all be wretched.' I agreed.

In one living room there's a muslin-covered tray, about 18 inches square, suspended from the ceiling. The director said: 'That is what we used to use as a refrigerator. We salted the food and hoped for the best.'

I remembered ice-boxes I had used as a youngster. On holiday in Canada, I had stayed in a house without a refrigerator. It had a large ice-box in the kitchen.

Every day the local ice merchant came and delivered the ice. In Sakhnin today, every house (Abdullah told me) has its refrigerator, its television and (in most cases) its car. Which is surprising, because the roads are so awful that the life expectancy of local cars must be very short.

Stephen Leacock, the well-known Canadian humorist of my youth, once said that if you want to get money from former pupils, do not show them new buildings. Show them instead the old rooms and preferably their own names carved into the woodwork of their old desks. So what entranced me most in the museum was a showcase with old money in it – a one pound note, from the Anglo-Palestine Bank, and a One Palestine Pound. I remember them. That shows that I am as old as the currency.

There is a souvenir shop in an upstairs room. Mainly ordinary. Nothing made in Sakhnin. The curator told me that they have no local handicrafts. None. So I bought my granddaughter Tali a silver necklace with a 'T' suspended from it. Probably made in Taiwan or Hong Kong.

Not even any postcards from Sakhnin. Only from 'the Arab World'. Jerusalem, Bethlehem, Nazareth – you name it and if it is in or near Israel, there are cards. No pictures of Sakhnin.

Abdullah steers me around. He is very friendly. Also, he is getting tired of speaking and repeating Arabic slowly and *my* still not understanding, so he prefers to speak English slowly, and repeating and then *my* not understanding – which is only fair, when you think about it. Meanwhile I'm putting Arabic words into the back of my notebook, along with ideas for this diary.

Another teacher of English introduces himself. Ibrahim Shaadi, who teaches in the village of Sha'ab, not far away. Would I like to visit him at home? Certainly I would. *Shukran* – thank you. We fix Wednesday at 11.30, when he finishes teaching. I would like to see another Arab town and get a different Arab point of view.

Chapter Five

ARIK RAZ

Until recently, Arik Raz was Chairman of the Regional Council of Misgav. This is the administrative area which includes Arab towns, from Kaukub to Deir Hana, from Manda to Sakhnin and which also takes in a larger scattering of Jewish towns and villages. I thought it would be a very good idea to meet him. 'To hear the other side', as David put it.

Arik arrived at the guest house at 5.30. He had lost his way and did not get the sort of warm help from local folk that I had received. I wondered why? Was it because in their eyes I was an Englishman while he was an Israeli Jew? Or had I found the right people to ask while he did not? Never mind. He got through eventually and Abdullah met him and brought him to the guest house and we sat outside at a white table on the patio, while Abdullah plied us with Arab sweetmeats, water-melon and iced orange juice. I decided that I would leave this place as well nourished as Abdullah and Jowdat.

I put to Arik the sort of points that local people had made to me, about their alleged ill treatment and discrimination at the hands of their Jewish fellow citizens. Here are Arik's answers:

No, the Israelis have not appropriated land around Sakhnin. Yes, they have bought some – but in Arik's view, not enough. There is plenty of room for building in and around Sakhnin. Their complaints about expropriation or appropriation are totally without foundation. The only possible justification was some 25 years ago, when some lands was expropriated when the town of Karmiel was established nearby. But that is all.

The villages on the top of the hill? The Jewish villages which they say were 'on their land'? Like the village of Esh'char which has about 100 families – and spectacular views across the valleys. I was looking at it from my side of the table.

Not true that it is on stolen land. It never was Arab land. It was unused land, owned by the Israel Land Authority.

'We bought it and you cannot stop history because you want to,' said Arik. 'This is one of the continuing quarrels we have with our Arab neighbours and we and they have to learn how to handle it.'

It is true that there is little contact between the inhabitants of Esh'char and those of Sakhnin. But it takes two hands to clap. And each body says that the other one does not provide the other hand.

Why has Sakhnin not got a swimming pool and recreational opportunities, whereas the Jewish towns have? In Misgav, where Arik lives, as in most other towns, they have these facilities because local people collect money for it and make it a priority. In Sakhnin, there is no such priority, and there are no collections and when you try to make an arrangement with them that you will match from taxes whatever they collect from citizens, they do not see why they should collect the money in the first place. Anyway (Arik said) the tax collection system in Sakhnin is rudimentary, unsatisfactory and doesn't work. There is little poverty here and many very attractive homes. But people do not pitch in for anything communal.

Why are there no gardens?

Because it is part of the culture that your house is your fortress and what matters is the inside and not the outside. He was quite surprised to see the patch of green at the end of the patio at the Shadi Guest House. Maybe six yards by fifteen.

They do not have recreational facilities because they do not create them. They do not have parks because it is not part of their culture. And they also collect no money at all from outside sources, like Jewish Israelis do. Like Gan Ner, the Janner village, for instance. Absolutely none whatever, ever.

What of the low level of crime among the youngsters? That is true. And it is also true that this is the result of the pressures of the *hamoula*. As for the low level of drugs – some hashish but little else, as I was told in the school – not quite true. Drugs are seeping in and are becoming something of a problem.

I asked Arik why it was that there were no Jewish visitors in Sakhnin.

'Well,' he said, 'It isn't exactly a tourist haven, is it? There is nothing much to do or to see.'

'Yes, but it is peaceful and friendly and different. And there is the museum and the town is a good base for visiting the north. Are Jewish people afraid of coming here?'

He thought for a moment. 'Yes, I suppose some are. They are apprehensive. But there is nothing to be afraid of. When you are a guest in an Arab house, you are safe.'

I told him that I thought it was much safer here than on Israel's roads. He told me that his eldest son is in the army in Lebanon. 'It's safer there, too, than on the Israeli roads,' I said.

'Yes. There is something in the Levantine psychology that makes our people drive like maniacs. So be careful when you drive here.' I am.

Some thoughts about local culture. Arik says that the Arab world works on the basis that if I do you a favour, you must expect to do me one, one day. You put the favour into the bank.

'So how can honest authorities cope with this?' I asked.

Sadly (he replied), this is very difficult to deal with, because, to misquote Churchill, so many owe so much to so many! That can stretch into areas of planning permission and of other sensitive problems and if a person owes something to someone else, the debtor feels obliged to pay off the debt to his moral creditor.

These differences, whether the absence of gardens or the presence of prime loyalties to parties rather than to places that you politically represent, go back to the cultures of the Levant. It is not a European approach, but Levantine. And you have to understand it if you are going to deal with it.

It means, for instance, that if you collect money, you prefer to spend it on political demonstrations for your party, not for creating facilities for your community. It means that if there is a party demonstration and also a trouble spot in your own town at the same time, the demonstration will be your priority. As mayor or other authority, to the demo you will go.

Arik agrees that because the leaders of Israel's Arab municipalities either are or are aspiring to be their national leadership, they must keep high profiles with the party. Nor are all the Jewish mayors above posturing.

Arik compared the totally different approach of my friend, Ijo Rager – mayor of Beersheba until he died of cancer just a week before. I had phoned David from London, to ask him to arrange for me to travel to see Ijo, who I knew was desperately ill. David made the arrangements – and then phoned me in London to say that he had heard on the radio that Ijo had died.

Ijo Rager, creator of the Soviet-Jewry movement in the United Kingdom. Ijo, whom Myra and I had lately joined in a crowded and proud tour of his Beersheba, where he had shown us how he had helped it to grow. Ijo, who put Beersheba before most else in his life. Well, sadly, most of the mayors of most of these towns are not like that, said Arik.

One exception: Ahmed Haj, mayor of Kawkab. It is only about a quarter of an hour away, and I must visit him.

We talked in English, Arik and I. Abdullah joined us and Arik talked to him in Hebrew. They discussed how difficult it is to build up a business like a guest house. 'It takes years,' says Arik. Abdullah explains how he wants Jewish people to come here. He is not interested in Arab business. He wants to make friendship with Jewish people.

When Arik had driven off – promising to put me in touch with the local chief of police – the children gathered round. More tricks?

I produced my special modelling balloons and made animals for them. They behaved like children do, anywhere in the world, fighting for who is going to be next and which coloured balloon they were going to have and when the balloon animals came apart would I do them another one and they had not had one and each one had to have another one and I nearly blew myself up and the balloons burst and that was the end of the party because I carefully had no more in my pocket.

Every time I thought I had finished blowing up balloons and my lungs were bursting, some other child would come up looking terribly miserable saying: 'One for me, one for me.' Which meant that she (usually) had not had one or that it was broken or that she wanted two. So I dug out some more balloons and went on bursting my lungs.

Jowdat insisted on blowing one up himself, and he would not let me do it for him and I told him it was very difficult. But he would not listen so I gave it to him and he could not blow it up and he came back, apologizing. And he had broken the balloon with his teeth. Good. So I did a lion for him and burst it when it was nearly complete, which taught me a lesson too.

Chapter Six

THE WEDDING

O h, what a privilege! But hell's bells, I have only got one spare pair of trousers and my lightweight grey ones are dirty and I wonder if they have any cleaners in town who will do it very quickly. We shall see tomorrow. I had better save my clean pair for Thursday's ceremony in Gan Ner.

Off to the wedding now – in the old dirty trousers – but in a crisp, clean, white shirt, which will make me feel a little better. And a shower first. Put on the switch, and in 20 minutes' time – *mumtaz* – hot water. Wonderful. I phoned Laura.

I have only been here a day and it seems like a week. And Thursday is massively full of new experience. Strange how when you are at home doing familiar tasks in familiar places with familiar people, the day streaks by. When you travel and fill your day with a new world, you and the day live longer. This, I realized, was a week crammed into 24 hours. Odd that they haven't cleaned my room or bathroom, or made my bed. I must find out why.

There is no other word for it – amazing. The wedding was amazing.

One of Abdullah's relatives took us in his car, with his wife Fawzieh. We drove through the town and I saw and heard a wedding. A band playing very loud Arab music, amplified and thumping, in a courtyard off the lower end of the high street. We didn't stop. Why? 'There are five weddings in town tonight and we are going to a different one. It is about six kilometres away.' Off we drove.

We arrived at a hall on a hill. Outside, there was an open space with a platform and, below it, rows of chairs, obviously for wedding ceremonies. But this ceremony, they said, had been conducted privately, in a house. Not like the Jewish ones, under the wide open canopies. But the celebration comes afterwards. Tonight.

I had presumed that it was a fairly simple affair. We would go into the hall and have a drink and maybe sit down and chat and then go. Abdullah was dressed in a shirt and slacks and open sandals, so I wore the same.

The hall was large, pale-coloured, with modern lighting, mirrored pillars, the band on a platform at one side and tables both on the lower level and raised, on the side opposite. Tables for about 400 people.

First, though, we joined a queue at the reception line, all smart, each in his or her own way. The women all in long dresses. And the local hairdressers had done well that day.

The men wore a variety of clothing. Some in suits and ties; some in shirts and and ties; some in open neck shirts; some even in jeans. But nobody except us, Abdullah and I, in open sandals. Myra would not have approved.

We shook hands with the groom, who I think recognized me from yesterday. He was dressed in a black suit with waistcoat and tie. The bride, in flowing white, with a sparkling tiara and necklace. Like all brides and queens in full regalia, she looked beautiful. A lock of hair fell neatly down each side of her well-rounded, smiling, dark face. The parents were alongside, one of the women wearing a white head covering. There was only one other woman in the room with the same. Then to a table, on the raised part of the hall.

The band was playing. People entered singly, or in pairs, or in small groups. The receiving line rose to greet them and rested as they moved on. We started nibbling.

The tables were covered with pink cloths, to match the chairs and the napkins. The hall was festooned with hanging leaves and pink flowers, all of them artificial. And the tables were loaded with a mix of oriental salads, and with pitta bread.

I had skipped lunch. Tea had been with Abdullah in a confectionery shop – marvellous Arab pastries, made with cheese and dates and all manner of calorific glories. Now, presuming that the salads were the evening's diet, I got stuck into them, and soon lost my hunger.

There were drinks on the table – in large plastic bottles, Pepsi Cola, orange, lemon, water . . . memories of the feast in Yemen, on the floor of the room in the palace of Sheikh Abdullah. All the brilliant food there was laid on a huge plastic tablecloth, replete with plastic bottles of cola and water. Whole roasted lambs and goats and piles of layered breads with honey and butter – and plastic bottles on a plastic cloth.

Here I learned my lesson on Sakhnin hospitality. The waiters carried in more food, at 8.30 and at five minute intervals after that until we left just before midnight. I thought of Myra. Her friends would have required details of the meal. I must be prepared to supply the same.

So – after the mixed salads, the waiters brought plates with more salads. All kinds. Then pastry triangles; then, heaped onto large, plastic type plates with the small ones on top, a great series of unexpected courses. Small half potatoes, well stuffed. 10.50: mixed fruits. 11.00: chips – delicious. 11.05: choice between barbecued chicken or steak. 11.10: rice. 11.15: peanuts in the shell. 11.20: more bread, more nuts.

What would have come later, I don't know, because we left at 11.45, before the sweetmeats and the coffee at the very least. But what a party it had been. *Hafla mumtaza* – a splendid feast. *Forsa sayida* – a great occasion.

The music throbbed. To my Western ear, it was full of urgent monotony. To the listeners, the audience, the smiling guests – it was a growing invitation to clap and to sway. First onto the dance floor came the women, graceful, arms at shoulder level, hands on high. All smiling. The men at the tables watched and clapped.

In the next session the women were joined by half a dozen brave men. By the end of the evening it was men only – swaying, clapping and jigging.

The groom had soon stripped off his coat, and he danced the evening away, with unrelenting energy. Around the dance floor and then around the tables, followed always by his troops of male supporters, clapping and laughing. One of them lifted him onto his shoulders and he made another triumphant round of the guests, waving, smiling, tossing greetings into the crowd.

Other friends – ushers, I presumed – moved around the tables with piled handfuls of packs of cigarettes, all open, urging them on the guests. Last night, a man had sprayed us with oriental scent, underneath our chins. This we were spared.

At one stage, the dance floor cleared and the bride and groom danced together. Alone. Bodies separate but eyes and smiles connected forever.

I missed Myra and walked into the car park with a cloud of smoke from above, and with the smell of charcoal fires. I knew then that the meal had hardly begun.

Back to the orchestra, the two singers' mouths close to the microphones. The violinist with his curiously shaped instrument. The mandolin with its swept-back neck. The modern keyboard playing popular, undulating Arab music. The audience, who knew all the tunes, clapped and swayed.

Watching the dancers, I thought of Harold Macmillan's marvellous advice to presenters – always make your gestures from the shoulder, never from the elbow or the wrist. The dancers moved from their shoulders. I took photographs with my throwaway camera.

I passed a young man with blondish hair. 'Shalom,' he said. 'I met you here last year.' 'Sorry,' I replied, 'this is only my second day in Sakhnin. It must have been someone else.' 'No it wasn't,' he said. 'I know you, you were here last year.'

One of his mates, asked: 'How are you? Are you enjoying it?' 'It's *mumtaz* – splendid. A great privilege for me. *Sharaftuni* – I am honoured.'

'*Shukran*,' he answered. 'Thank you.'

'*La shukr allal wajib*,' I replied, in my best Arabic. 'Do not thank me for doing my duty.'

A young man in a white shirt and tie, and with a gold chain with a charm hanging around his neck, smiled at me. 'Welcome,' he said, in English. Then, in Arabic: '*Marhaban*.' I thanked him. I had seldom felt more welcome in my life.

There was high tech, too. A console with several TV sets and a man sitting all evening pushing buttons up and down and switching screens. Two men with TV cameras on their shoulders and powerful floodlights in one hand, up and down the room, filming and recording hosts and guests and the band and food and laughter and songs.

There was an official photographer. He took a photograph of Abdullah and myself, at Abdullah's request. As usual, Abdullah would not let me pay for it when it appeared. He told the photographer who I was and the photographer came over later and introduced himself.

'I am a new immigrant, from Kiev,' he said, in perfect English.

'So what are you doing in Sakhnin?'

'Earning my living. I have to live!'

He was middle-aged, nondescript in pale clothing and he soon vanished into the crowd. By then I was rapidly and literally getting cold feet so I decided to stand up and move around. Abdullah took me firmly by the wrist. 'We dance,' he said.

We moved towards the dance floor, with the bride and groom gyrating in the centre of the crowd. I stayed on the edge and clapped in rhythm.

Three little bridesmaids in white were dancing nearby, together with a small boy. It could have been a Jewish wedding. If they had changed the music to our Jewish monotony. The band played one song which had almost the same melody as a song by Rabbi Carlebach. My daughter, Marion, and I had enjoyed him at the wedding of David Susskind's daughter, in Brussels, many years ago.

More music, more food, more clapping, more smiles, more greetings. Air-conditioned and joyful happiness: a privilege indeed. *Sharaftuni*.

At about 11.45, my host stood up. 'Ready to go?'

'Up to you. I'm happy to stay all night.'

'Well, we've got work tomorrow. So *yalla* – let's go.'

We walked out, waving our thanks to the host, the groom, the friends – and to a fantastic evening – especially for the bride, the groom, and me.

During the drive home, the two couples chatted and chattered in Arabic and I understood only an occasional word. They switched on the radio for more loud and happy music. It was lucky we could not talk over dinner. The music had been much too loud. And when they could not hear me and I could not hear them, that saved us multi-lingual embarrassment.

I was disappointed that I could understand so little of their conversation and I told them so. 'No problem,' they replied. 'We are talking *amiya* – local dialect.'

Home to bed. Plug in one of the uneaten Spira mats. Close the mosquito blinds and open the windows to get some air. Read a chapter of John Grisham's *The Partner*. Then to sleep.

Zoom. Zoom. Zoom, the mosquito dive bomber had arrived. I checked the windows. I had not closed the blind over one of the open ones.

I opened the bathroom door and left the light on in the forlorn hope that the mosquito would burn itself out on the bulb. No such luck. Twice during the night it was back.

I am awake so I might as well write this story in my bedroom. A cockroach has just run across the floor. I must squelch it – which I do. It's the second one I've seen today. The other caused greater laughter at the museum, when the director was demonstrating an implement to plant one melon seed at a time and he lifted the tube and out fell a cockroach. Yuk!

The Shadi Guest House is spotlessly clean. I cannot imagine why any cockroach would bother visiting it.

Eventually, the mosquito sleeps, and so do I.

Chapter Seven

IN TOWN

Woke at 8. Phoned Laura. It is as hell-fire hot in Jerusalem as it is in Sakhnin and I wish she would let me put air-conditioning into the children's room. That would give me real pleasure. We shall see. To be precise: Laura will see.

Finally got through to Ahmed Haj, mayor of the nearby town of Kawkab. Will visit him this afternoon.

Breakfast on the patio and magic, laughter and Arabic with Jowdat. The same delicious green herb omelette and excellent salads as yesterday. The birds chattered merrily in their cage. Noticed at the foot of the tree some rusty scythes, same as in the museum.

This life is totally unreal, surreal, removed from any other place or time in my life. Until I receive a fax. I am to phone my godson, accountant and friend, Nigel, on urgent business. All magic is illusion and the spell is broken. But not for long.

Our neighbour drove me to the Artist's House, at the top of the hill. Jowdat came with me. We stopped outside the house opposite and the man who emerged said that he would get the key, but meanwhile please would we do him the honour of coming into his home.

Our host and Jowdat sat on the rusty remains of a garden swing – especially dangerous to the tiny child tottering nearby. Two other chairs and cups of sweet coffee and the man told us that his father was the priest in the church. They lived very happily here, the Christians. They are only about five per cent of the town's population. No problem. No differences. Would I like to see the church? It is Greek Orthodox.

The church is small, ornate, with high, wooden straight-backed pews and pictures of the Virgin Mary on the walls. A small vestry, with colourful vestments hanging over the table. Our host's father was the man in white I had met on the first night of the wedding celebration. He was proud of the place. I took his photograph inside the building and outside in the narrow, shining street.

Then we got the key to the Artists' House and wandered around. The artist in charge was away and our host knew little about it. A pleasant interlude, but nothing more. Another wasted attraction, for those neglected and invisible tourists.

Back to the house opposite. A three-story building and our new friend's flat was on the top floor. A marvellous view from the balcony, across the whole valley and up to the mountains on either side.

The living room was in traditional style, which means seating all round the edges – the sides and the corners and the alcoves – so that the maximum number of people can sit in comfort and look at each other. No chairs or couches criss-crossed or tables to take away the sense of space. And open windows on both sides, to maximize the breeze.

Coffee and water – water, which I was told was as safe to drink as that in Jerusalem or London and probably safer. And do come back. *Merhaban* – welcome.

Sakhnin is not a town where people sit at cafés and chat and drink coffee and play *shishbish*, or backgammon by whatever name. Which is just as well, because you are filled with coffee everywhere you walk. Everywhere you enter. Everywhere that you do not want to be rude and say no.

Our next stop, for coffee and talk, was at the municipality. Dr Qasem Aburaya works there. He is Director of Strategic Planning.

The building is modest and the people friendly and I noted a man in blue trousers which were much too long for him, in a fat body supporting a bald head, nodding his way down the corridor, looking totally bored. We sat and waited while they called Qasem. He was at home on leave. Within five minutes, he came in.

A smiling man, who expressed the highest regard for our David, whom he knew well – which, of course, endeared him to me immediately. He told us the problems with their strategic planning. The main one: to plan, you need money. They have very little. He tries to get the municipality to look ahead, but there is too much owing from behind. So much so that the staff have not had their wages paid for the last four months. That is why they went on strike. But that did not do any good.

'How do you all manage?'

He shrugged. 'My wife works and my overdraft is growing and so is the interest charged on it. But I suppose it will be all right one day.'

'Do people pay their taxes here?' I ask.

'That is a problem. People do pay less than the Jews. But income tax is deducted from wages. The real trouble is that as a municipality, we get only about a third of the sum the Jewish towns get. The gap is narrowing, but not by much. We have to work out what we have and it is not enough to pay the salaries.'

'What are your real problems, other than salaries – and roads,' I ask.

'Fifty per cent of Sakhnin is not connected to the sewerage system.'

'So what do you do when you build new houses?'

'We dig new holes.'

'Who is the government minister responsible?'

'The Minister of Internal Affairs, Eliyahu Suisa.'

'Perhaps I can make a case to him. You never know.'

'We only have less than two million shekels for all our development projects,' says Qasem. 'That is less than £400,000 sterling for a year. What can we do with that? Well, we try to strengthen the economic base for our town. David used to do that with us. He has moved on but is still in touch, which is good. But our best is not very good. We try.'

I let the man go back to his holiday and we agree that on Friday morning we will try to go for a stroll together and just chat.

'*Shukran*,' I say, '*La shukr allal wajib*,' he replies. When people here say that it is an honour or duty for which they should not be thanked, they give you the feeling that they mean it.

Chapter Eight

THE CHIEF OF POLICE

The chief of police of Misgav is a 50-year-old, medium height, balding man called Efraim Solomon. Born in Romania, he came to Israel as a youngster and volunteered to live in a Shomer Hatsair, left-wing kibbutz called Ain Dor, where (as he told me) they made no distinction between people because of their origins and religions.

The Misgav police station is about five minutes from Sakhnin. Just up the road. Proud of my pioneering self, my car and I found our own way to the police car park and I was allowed in through the sliding steel gates. Efraim was emerging from his car, pistol on hip. Yes, he was expecting me. Please do come inside.

In his small, air-conditioned office, we chatted for an hour and a half. At first, he was interrupted by phone calls. Later, he switched the phone off and warmed to his subject and to me.

He tells me that I must understand the culture and the traditions of the Arabs in the area, or I will not know anything. In most places, they are built on the *hamoula* – the extended family. That is good in some ways. In others, especially in political life, it can be very bad. If you are elected mayor because your *hamoula* is the largest in town, and whether on your own or in coalition with a smaller one you run the place, then your *hamoula* will expect favours. I do a favour for you and you do one for me and I put mine in the bank and expect you to redeem it when I want it.

That means better roads and planning permissions and a hospital near your *hamoula*, not somewhere else. It also means that instead of working with the town's interest paramount, you have to look after your *hamoula*.

This reminded me of the disputes between tribes in the Yemen. Like the time that one tribe kidnapped French tourists because the authorities had diverted the road which was to have passed through their territory along a different route, because the Minister responsible belonged to a tribe that wanted the road to pass through his area. As with Yemeni tribes, so with Israeli Arab *hamoulas*.

Still, the *hamoula* is not what it was. In the old days, its head was the power unit and you used to have to do what he told you. Not any more. Yet there is still respect.

Good does come from the *hamoula*. But it also creates the greatest problem – battles between families. Which means not just fists but also sometimes bottles with petrol and rags, and sometimes hundreds or even thousands of people involved in fighting. When the police come in, it is dangerous for them. At least no one has kidnapped foreign tourists, to make their point.

A couple of weeks ago, Efraim was called in to an interesting *hamoula* battle. He tried to find out what was happening. They did not realize that it was his car, but simply stoned it. It is dented all over. Dangerous. It can all start with two youngsters from school, each from a different *hamoula*, having a row and a fight and each goes home and tells his parents and they call out the *hamoula* 'troops' and the 'battle' is on.

In both Jewish and Arab towns, mayors are elected. In Jewish towns, the mayors have to be active and when it comes to the next elections they will be called to account. It is not the same with the Arabs. Elections are democratic. But it is the *hamoulas* who decide who wins.

In some local towns – like Kawkab and Deir Hana – the mayors do a first-class job. But then in Kawkab at least, there is only one *hamoula*.

'I don't know whether it is true that these towns get less money from central government than the Jewish ones,' he says. 'That is not my department. But if it is true, can you please tell me why it is that Kawkab, for instance, has excellent roads and facilities and Sakhnin has not?'

I thought of Qasem Aburaya, who had told me this morning that 'our management is not perfect'. Perhaps that was an understatement.

Crime? Well there is some in all the Arab towns. In Kawkab, very little. Not much in Deir Hana and not too bad in Sakhnin either.

Why is this? Well, it goes back to the *hamoulas*. The youngsters are afraid to commit crimes in their own place. If, for instance, they want to steal in their own town, and they are found in someone else's home, the owner will probably think that the intruder has come to bed his wife and may knife him for his welcome. So instead, they go off to Akko and Haifa and Karmiel to do their stealing. 'It is dignity. It is respect. You don't foul your own nest.' My daughter Marion, who worked for the National Association for the Care and Rehabilitation of Offenders (NACRO), calls it 'displacement'.

Then there is the curious problem of alcohol and drugs, and here you have to understand the culture. If, for instance, you go to some of these towns, you will find young people outside the boundaries, drinking beer and throwing the bottles away. They do not do it at home.

When they get home, there is nothing much to do except watch television and they cannot get alcohol. So some of them take drugs. But it is older people who sell drugs in the Arab villages. In the Jewish towns, it is too often the young ones.

Much of this has to do with religion. Ninety-five per cent of the Arabs are religious and they avoid doing what is forbidden, in their own town.

Another example: Efraim tries to get someone important to start a community centre in an Arab town. 'Do you want to get me killed?' the man protests. 'You can't have a community centre just for boys or just for girls. And to mix them is forbidden' – in the towns.

Which explains why last night's joyful wedding party – with men and women dancing together and with beer on the tables – was held far outside the boundaries of Sakhnin.

Efraim tries to get schools to keep their buildings and play areas open after school hours. The teachers tell me that the youngsters will take the footballs. I say: 'Good. They are not taking them because they want to steal them but because they want to play with them. So why not open the place up?' Not without money, say the teachers.

There are no football fields. Land for parks and gardens? You will not get them because people want houses and if you look at the mess in Sakhnin, you will find that streets are narrow and winding and, especially where the local *hamoula* is not in power, in poor condition. In Kawkab, it is different. 'It's priorities, isn't it?'

I suggest that it is also land. Who owns it?

'People here have to understand that we do not have enough water and land for food. So instead of building villas on fertile ground, they should do what you do in England and America and build up. High-rise flats. They will not do it, because everybody wants a villa. So there is no space for gardens and recreation.'

Curiously, high-rise flats in Britain produce the same problems. No gardens and nowhere for children and people to play. And this is a problem as much for the Jews in Israel as for its Arabs. Israel is over-urbanized – no 'green belts' but plenty of traffic congestion and the pollution that goes with it.

'There is a problem with communication too. Of course the Bedouin would prefer to roam what they call their ancient lands. But it cannot happen in a modern state. You cannot leave land empty for most of the year and even then scarcely filled. People have to adapt and it is very difficult for them and this we must understand. It is a cultural problem. We must give them help and they must understand.'

All these problems tend to settle down most of the time but the real anger flares up at election time or just before it. Yes, there are Arabs and Jews in the police and they work very closely and well together. Efraim sees to that. But you also have to train the policemen to understand.

'We all have to learn,' says Efraim. 'Learning is a slow process. Remember that the Arabs have more respect for learning than the Jews.' Which reminds him of an Arabic saying which I remember better in English: Stand up for your teacher and give him respect, for the teacher is almost a prophet.

Efraim tells me a long story about how he had gone into a Jewish school and they all had their feet up and the teacher was writing on the blackboard and he had said that it was disrespectful, and the teacher said, 'What can you do?' So he showed her what he could do and he talked to them for two hours and they listened in silence. Then he answered their questions, most of them about the police. No one had their feet up on the desks.

Anyway, there is more crime of all sorts among the Jews in his area. And more truancy, too – although Arab truancy is beginning to get worse.

'I've learned that all people are equal, but it is the minority that cause the trouble and make the noise.' He picked up a box. 'Look, if I put two stones into this box and shake it they will make a big noise. But if I fill it up with stones and pack them in, it is all quiet. It's the same with people. Get the majority together and they are silent. What we have to do is to induce the majority to speak up.

'Remember that there is a strong and good wish from all sides to have peace. Now is the time for peace. As you say in English, the iron is hot, so strike with it. Do not let those who make the noise break it. And do not lose the moment.'

Every few minutes, Efraim paused and pointed at the map on the wall. 'Here is the Jewish area. It is not true to say that Jews have expropriated Arab land. It is owned by the state unless you have bought it and if you have bought it it is yours. And if you haven't bought it and would like it, that's rough.

'They do have land to build in Sakhnin. It's just that they want other land and they don't use the land they have properly. And instead of using political money for building in a sensible way, they use it for demonstrations.'

I realized that I was touching, literally and metaphorically, both politically and historically sensitive ground. On the one hand, some argue that the Zionists bought land legitimately, from absentee landowners, mainly Ottomans, but not from Palestinians. The Palestinians have not held title deeds for the land, though, it was passed down from generation to generation, through the *hamoula*. No papers needed.

Then the British set up systems of land registration which, some argue, was unfair on the Palestinians.

We have to deal with today, though. With the reality of here and now and of the future, and where do we go from here and what is the role of history in the future of peace?

As I chewed his tasty plums and apples and nibbled his biscuits and cake and drank iced water and coffee, I thought how fortunate Sakhnin was to be in an area with such an intelligent chief of police as Efraim. But what a burden of sensitivity he must bear.

At 3. pm, I was meant to speak to the mayor of Kawkab. Efraim phoned him for me. He asked the mayor why he did not start building a factory to make beer without alcohol. 'You'd be rich. Just think how many Muslims would drink it, and how many Jews too.' Then he introduced me and the mayor confirmed: 5 pm at the municipality.

Just time to find my way home, through the curling, narrow streets of Sakhnin, stopping at the nearby supermarket for that cherished ice-cream, for all the family. I knew their tastes by now.

Last time ice-cream came by their house was in the morning. A man carrying two sacks over his shoulders passed by, shouting. 'Who's he?' I asked. 'He's the supermarket!' they laughed. 'Ice-creams or anything else you want, just ask him . . .' The one up the road had a better stock.

When 'Supermarket' had safely passed out of sight, I went for a contemplative stroll. How can we harness the power of laughter, to overcome suspicion and dislike?

Bob Monkhouse is my humour hero. The essence of his rules is simple. If you use humour, it must both suit you and your style. You must feel comfortable with it and it must amuse you. If you do not think it is funny, avoid it.

Equally important: it must suit your audience. You vary your humour to suit that audience. Above all and by far the most important rule: humour must not offend. If you offend your audience, you are dead.

If follows that you must avoid racist jokes or stories. Be careful with sex and with politics. Those are the 'do nots'. The 'do' is simpler – make fun of yourself. If you tease yourself, no one else will be upset.

So I use a store of stories about lawyers and politicians. I enjoy telling Jewish tales. But I rarely joke about other people's jobs or nationalities and never about their race or religions.

Most stories are easily adaptable. For instance, there was a mythical 19th-century Jewish town in Poland, called Chelm. The inhabitants were all very stupid. Like the man who wanted light in his home so he went out at night with a bucket and when it was filled with moonlight, he covered it up with a cloth and took it back inside his house and was amazed to find it dark and empty.

How, then, can you recognize the modern man from Chelm, in a car-wash? He is the one on the motor-bike.

That is fine. But it would not be if you are English and the butt of the joke is an Irishman; if you are Canadian, and the victim is a

'Newfie' – a man from Newfoundland; or a Russian and you tell the story about a Pole . . .

What do you call a bus, half-filled with lawyers, which crashes from the top of a cliff into the sea? A waste of the other half. Fine for me. But if I substitute someone else's profession for my own, I will offend.

I would never tell jokes or make wisecracks about Arabs. I did not know the Halayles well enough even to tell jokes about the British or the Jews, about politicians or lawyers. Nor could I have coped in my Arabic or their Hebrew, nor would they have understood the nuances in our shared English.

Word play – jeux de mots – that is the basis of much wit and laughter. To succeed, both the teller and the audience must know the language well. Which ruled it out for me, at the Shadi Guest House.

We were left, then, with human frailty – our own. My clumsy tongue . . . Abdullah's rickety car . . . Sakhnin's potholed roads . . . and 'Supermarket' – the house-to-house vendor, loaded down with a mighty weight of assorted, basic human needs.

Chapter Nine

THE HAMOULA

I have researched the *hamoula* – the extended family. I have discussed it carefully and realized that it is not simply an Arab concept. When I was surrounded by it in Sakhnin, I recognized it both from the Jewish and from the Indian worlds.

Even today, Jews who organize a family party often find that by the time they have invited their fourth cousins, twice removed – who are probably as close to them as most people's first cousins unremoved – they either need to book the Royal Albert Hall, or face that special Jewish upset, known as 'broigus' – which you can define in the context of the *hamoula* as not being invited to an extended family gathering.

For the Indian community in Leicester, the *hamoula* was and remains a much more serious issue. I met it immediately I was an elected Member of Parliament for what was then Leicester North West. Idi Amin was on his racist rampage in Uganda. A few hundred Asians had arrived in our city, seeking refuge, homes and work. As they settled in, their *hamoula* followed them.

The Asians came largely from a cluster of villages, near the Gujarat capital of Ahmedabad. The first arrivals brought their parents and brothers and sisters, their uncles and aunts and cousins.

Prime Minister Edward Heath honourably recognized that even though these persecuted people were not British citizens, with a right to settle in the UK, they were 'British passport holders'. As such, we had a moral duty to receive them.

Gradually, the number of Leicester Asians crept up. People asked me: 'Why Leicester?' Answer: the *hamoula*. Your cousins arrive from your village. Where would they go? To your home, of course. Where will they stay? In your home, of course, until they find somewhere else. You are not going to let members of your extended family go without a roof over their heads, are you? So the numbers of Asians in Leicester crept up, like human compound interest.

In 1972, the Leicester City Council decided that they could absorb no more immigrants. They were worried about possible racial problems and actual housing shortage and unemployment. So they took the only step which could absolutely guarantee an immediate and unremitting flood of *hamoula* into the city. They put an advertisement in newspapers, in Uganda's capital, Kampala. They pleaded: 'Do not come to Leicester. Our city is overcrowded. There will be no facilities for you. Please go somewhere else.'

Uganda's intelligent Leicester Asians immediately telephoned their Ugandan *hamoula*. 'Hurry,' they said. 'Come now. Don't wait. Don't you see – these adverts show that soon they will close the gates of the city, and you will not get in?'

So come they did, by their thousands. A whole series of terraced houses in my constituency, leading into the major Belgrave Road, became 90 per cent Asian. The area became known as 'Little India'. Belgrave Road turned into a mighty Indian shopping centre and a magnet for Asians from all over the Midlands, especially on their great festivals of Diwali and Navratri.

Today, some 30 per cent of Leicester's citizens are Asian. They have brought colour and industry and employment into what was once the second wealthiest city in Europe but whose stability had foundered, along with the growth of imports of our staple manufactured products – hosiery, knitwear and footwear.

The *hamoulas* demanded education for the children. A teacher in one disadvantaged area of my patch told me: 'The Asian influx has brought new intelligence into my school.' Leicester's Asian *hamoula* demand that their young people study hard at school, work hard in their jobs and respect their elders.

As in Sakhnin, so in Leicester – the power of the *hamoula* is starting to ebb away. But it remains a mighty and largely unrecognized source of civic strength.

The *hamoula* must also deal with tolerance and racism directed against its members. As in Sakhnin, so in Leicester – the community tends to spend its social life at least, in its own, safe bubble. But in Leicester, it has spread its influence out into industrial, commercial and political worlds. Lord Mayors, politicians, industrialists, shop-keepers and voluntary workers – Leicester citizens. They work together and with others.

It was in 1972 that I called my first meeting of the Leicester Asian community. They had no temples or meeting places of their own, so we gathered in a church hall. A man in a traditional white Indian dhoti stood up and said: 'Mr Janner, you have talked to us about racism. What do you know about it? You do not know what it is to be discriminated against because of your colour. You do not know what it is like to be spat on because you are not white. Do not preach to us about fighting racism.'

'Oh yes, I know about racism,' I answered. 'I am a Jew and half my family were wiped out because of their race. Sadly, I am a great expert on this subject. One of my jobs now is to make sure that you and your families do not face the same fate.

'We have the same enemies. Now let us work together to defeat them.'

From then on, that is precisely what we did.

My Asian friends adopted me as an honorary Gujarati. It was my honour to promote and to defend their rights, alongside those of all my other constituents. Their *hamoula* was mine.

A distinguished Indian High Commissioner addressed a vast meeting in my constituency. He told them: 'Do not rely on your success or your wealth to give you the security that you need. You must get out and serve your city.' As a Jew, I saluted him. No one knows better than we Jews that success or prominence, whether in the arts or business or in any other sphere of prowess, cannot ensure your security. You must move out from your *hamoula*, and give service.

This I found, was one of the main problems in Sakhnin. Members of a *hamoula* will serve their families and sometimes their city. But voluntary service and the creation of community organizations and structures, is not an area in which their custom has taught them to excel. *Li soo' al hath* – alas. *Hamoulas* which wish to survive must turn outwards and not simply flourish within.

I admired and related to my hosts' family values. To them, it was home and children before all else, followed by the extended family.

I thought of the day when my father decided not to stand again for his Leicester West seat. Legend had it that he deliberately stood down so close to the 1970 election that the local Labour Party had already printed its posters: 'JANNER FOR LABOUR', and had to select me because they could not afford a reprint!

Unfortunately, the truth was different. My father was 76 but had every intention of carrying on in the Commons until he dropped dead in harness. His doctor decreed otherwise and told him that if he took part in an election campaign, there could be no guarantee that he would be alive at the end of it.

So I got called into my parents' home. Father told me his decision and asked whether I would like to have my name go forward, as a possible candidate for selection.

I went straight home to Myra and she said: 'It's a very important decision. I need to think about it.'

That night, she was washing the dishes and I was drying them. Before the days of our dishwasher, this chore was a joint family function. Myra turned to me. 'I've decided,' she said.

'What's your decision, darling?'

'Let's do it. But together. And on terms.'

'What are the terms?'

'That you will continue taking the children to school every morning. And that you will not seek ministerial office.'

Myra knew that our morning school rota runs were important to the children. What she did not want was a repeat of the relationship which I had with my father. He was still asleep when I left home each morning and I was asleep before he got home in the evening.

As for 'seeking office', we had too many friends whose marriages had collapsed under the weight of their red despatch boxes and the awful working hours that Ministers endure. Myra did not want to spend her life on her own.

I was happy with the terms and not only accepted them at the time, but kept to my side of that family bargain.

Politicians of all parties talk about 'family values'. Most important, without question, is the time that you spend with your children. Abdullah and Fawzieh build their lives around their three youngsters. That was one reason why I felt (literally) so at home, with the five of them.

I wandered through most parts of Sakhnin. Of course, there was poverty and need, especially among the elderly and the ill. But the *hamoula* looks after its own.

In Leicester, I learned the Indian tradition of caring for and respecting the elderly. Our Asians do not allow their aged relatives to be looked after in old people's homes. That is a family disgrace. Instead, they are cherished in the homes of their children. So it is in Sakhnin. We have much to learn from them.

I wondered how parents and children survived the emotional world of at least three generations in one crowded home. With every love possible, each generation needs its privacy, its space and its independence. Admittedly, you get few of those essentials in most homes for the elderly. My children need not worry. Love them as I do, I shall not live with them. Not for me, the *Hamoula for the Aged*.

Nor is there in Sakhnin the grim level of poverty that I have too often met in so many other countries, both inside and without the Arab world. No hungry children. No hutments or shacks or people living on the streets. None of the startling contrasts of staggering wealth and beauty, set against the grim depths of deprivation.

In India, I have watched, with wonder and delight, magnificent wedding processions, with bride and groom in glorious robes bedecked with jewels. Alongside, there was poverty, deep and dreadful.

In Cairo, you can bask in the golden glories of King Tutankhamen and be received with modern hospitality in homes and hotels among the world's most comfortable. Then you walk through horrible slums. Like the ones near the ruins of the Maimonides Synagogue, which crumble alongside the tiled remains of the seminary, where that great sage taught his disciples, some nine centuries ago.

It was there that I visited an ancient and half-crazed Jewish woman, living upstairs in a decrepit, two-storey block, with her room and the balcony cluttered with plastic bags of rubbish. Cairo once boasted a wealthy and cultured Jewish community. Today there are only about 85 left, most of them elderly ladies.

I noticed in the Cairo slums that I was received with much greater, more smiling warmth than in the better-off areas. I was not altogether surprised, because India's slum dwellers are almost universally friendly to visitors.

A wise and independent-minded Egyptian friend told me that the most vehement opposition to Israel and to the Peace Process comes from middle-class people and from intellectuals, aged between 55 and 65. They were brought up during the Nasser era.

They speak only one language – their own. They have not travelled and broadened their minds. They are poor (he said) in both pocket and perception. Just the type of disadvantaged and bitter middle-class males who put Hitler into power.

I hope the next generation will be different and will welcome diversity. For instance, no Egyptian I met wants war, but real peace means living together in goodwill – as I did, in Sakhnin. The Egyptian authorities have always, at the least, frowned on their people visiting Israel, even while Israelis were pouring into the land of the Pyramids, the Sphinx and Luxor, of the coral waters of Ras Muhammed and the biblical glories of Santa Katarina, on Mount Sinai itself. How sad.

When I last visited Cairo, the atmosphere towards Israelis and Jews – and they do not generally make much distinction between the two – was fragile and taut, a direct reflection of the current state of the Middle East Peace Process. But my reception in the slums was happy. Why? Because, my Egyptian Jewish hosts told me, poor people do not read newspapers. The better-off imbibe the newsprint hatred. The poor may watch television, but the venom is usually less than in the printed word. 'The poor don't hate like the rich,' they said.

In Sakhnin, the contrasts are blurred. The average family in Sakhnin has an income perhaps twenty times as high as their counterparts in Egypt.

As a young man, I spent a year at Harvard Law School, studying criminology. I visited prisons all over the United States. One of the questions I always asked was: 'How do you avoid trouble from prisoners?' The answer was generally the same: 'If they are happy with the food, they will put up with almost everything else.'

In Sakhnin, they are happy with the food. True, the food at the wedding feast was simple, but it was abundant and delicious, and served to their Jewish guest with radiant urging to keep eating.

'Ess' – eat. That was the first word I had learned in the Yiddish language. On the first anniversary of the liberation of the Belsen concentration camp, I had attended the tearful, distressful ceremony at the Jewish memorial, and then been invited to tea at the Kinderheim – the Children's Home. Thirty waifs were dressed in clothes cut from khaki US Army blankets. The food was festive by their standards, horrendous by mine. Dry bread, herring, milkless tea. 'Gavriel, ess,' they commanded me. Those with little give much.

Next Yiddish words: 'Shpilstie ping-pong?' Which, I worked out, was an invitation to play, which we did and that sealed what became in many cases a lifelong friendship. And so, I am sure, will my friendship prove with at least some of my new Sakhnin friends. Certainly, with the family at the Shadi Guest House. They have extended their family to include me. We belong to the same sector of the human family. Our diversity is the main source of our interest, each to the other, based as it is on a sense of shared heritage and cultural commonality.

Chapter Ten

MAYOR AND TOMB

Off to see the mayor of Kawkab, in my trusty, rusty Cavalier. To my great and smug self-satisfaction, I find the route to the main road and turn off to the right. About five minutes later, I think I have gone the wrong way. I pull in at a nearby town and ask a lad, 'Where's Kawkab?' I do it in my best Arabic. He replies, first in Hebrew. Then he smiles broadly and says in English: 'Are you from Britain?' So much for my Arabic. He then tells me that I am going the opposite way. So much, too, for what my mother called 'my bump of direction'.

I arrive at Kawkab at 4.45. 'Where is the mayor?' 'Follow me,' says a driver, smiling. I do. We end up on the outskirts of the village, outside a fine-looking house, with children and young people sprawling about. I get out of the car and ask for Ahmed Haj. A young man, who turns out to be his son, an architect trained in Russia, tells me that I have come to his home, not to his office. He telephones his father, who says: 'Never mind, I'll come home too.' Which he does.

The mayor is a tall, bronzed, young-looking man, charming and straight-spoken. He is tired, at the end of his day.

He tells me that Kawkab is easier to handle than Sakhnin because it is one-tenth the size. But yes, he projects forward and others do not. If he has even a little money to spare, then he plans to start a project. Like the swimming pool. They must have one. That will start next year.

No, not one person from Kawkab has gone out into the world and made money and is able to come back and contribute to the quality of life in the village. Some are abroad now, but they are too young. The village has to rely on its own resources.

Yes, they get much less than the Jewish villages. Why? 'Because we are not equal citizens and we never have been. It is a bit better than it was. But Peres did not do enough when he could and now we have the Netanyahu government.

'Ninety-five per cent of people in the village voted for Peres. Still, we have got to make the best of it and we do.'

It is not true that they collect less taxes than they should, either nationally or for the municipality. They just have less money. But in Kawkab they use it better than in most towns.

The mayor is trying to create a club and a football field and facilities for the young. It is easier in Sakhnin, in a sense, because youngsters there usually have access to a car and they go off to Akko or Haifa for the fun of it. There are not so many well-off young people in Kawkab.

In came his wife with the inevitable coffee and water, plus cold, sweet water-melon. I did magic for his little niece – which pleased the 16-year-old and his friend more than it did the child.

The mayor told me that he was coming to England in November on a course. He will of course be vastly welcome when he comes and I look forward to seeing him.

In between, there were phone calls and youngsters moving in and out. It was not fair to stay longer. So I asked the way back home, and his younger son and his friend climbed into the car and we wound our way through the village – noticeably better planned and with better roads than Sakhnin.

Back home at Shadi, it was faxes and business phone calls – the magic mirror was again smashed.

Supper in the garden with Shaaban Shaleh, the neighbour. He is *zaalan* – 'gefruntzled' – upset. He teaches Arabic and speaks perfect English and had offered to help me. Why had I not come to him? So I take him at his word and he translates into Arabic a list I had completed of common words which I did not know.

For a 'bed and breakfast', this hospitality must be unknown in the world. Salads, chicken, rice garnished with nuts, orange juice and soft drinks. All on the patio.

Then Abdullah said: 'Please come with me. I want to show you beautiful things, in the Old Town.'

He clattered his car over the slopes and into and out of the bumps and at the top of the hill it coughed and stalled. Three cars coming in three directions and all with no room to pass anyone anywhere. This must be one of the most unplanned cities in the world. And God knows when the rubbish was last collected – no one else does. They just say: 'Ah, we collect every week but people throw stuff down on the pavements. *Khalas* – what the hell? There's nothing we can do about it so there's no point in getting upset, is there?'

We stopped outside the Artist's House. This time the artist was there in person. He had all the extra postcards I had paid for on my previous visit, and a batch more, which he wanted to give me as a gift. Admittedly they are the only ones I have found with the word Sakhnin on them, but most are grotesque and frightening – entirely unsuitable. An open-mouthed horror of a young man, screaming . . . a beautiful woman with too many breasts . . . two women, with three breasts between them and an extra head . . . But there are some pleasant ones, with olive trees, some with faces, some without. All the work of the artist himself – Mahmud Badarny. He is certainly talented and I hope people will buy his talent before it is too late and the Artist's House closes down. My contribution will not keep him going long, but it is a start, I suppose.

Badarny – a tall, cadaverous man – told me that he came from Sakhnin and went to Holland. He left his wife and child there and returned three years ago. The municipality promised him that they would exhibit his pictures at no charge, but they have not done so. They have broken their word. Well, he is managing now.

I bought two prints from him, framed – ten pounds sterling each, including the frame. He threw in eight other prints, which he signed for me – as a gift. I left another ten pound note on the table and he protested. Abdullah said to me: 'If you have any problem with money, I will give you whatever you need. You are my guest.' Which I am quite sure he meant, and I am going to have problems when it comes to paying my bill at the end of my stay.

Abdullah said he wanted to show me other high spots of the Old Town, at night.

I told him I was very tired, wilting from the hospitality, the heat and the activity. But let's go for a walk for a while. We climbed back into his car, chuntering and leaping and bounding over the potholes, to the top of the old city, under the shade of the mosque. With its minaret – a magnificent, white, still, pointed finger, on the corner of a fine edifice. Inside, three men were reading from the Koran, cross-legged and stooped forward. A wooden pulpit. A fine exterior, simple within.

We got out of the car and strolled along the streets, with cries of '*Ahlain*' and '*Merhaben*'. And '*Kayf Halak*' – how are you? – as Abdullah passed each group of people on the balcony of their white stone houses, or sitting below and drinking coffee. They knew him and he knew them all and we waved and so did they.

Then down some steps and onto a small, rubbish-strewn courtyard – perhaps ten feet by five. '*Shoof*. Look,' said Abdullah, flashing his torch on an inscription of the doorway of a solemn, squat building. The letters were in Hebrew. They read: Rabbi Yehoshua of Sakhnin.

'The Rabbi lived here about 1600 years ago,' Abdullah said. 'A wise man. A sage.'

We inched inside. A sarcophagus with pointed ends and the lid askew, half-filled with torn cigarette packets and sand and muck. Henna painted onto one end. 'Brides come here because they think it's lucky,' said Abdullah. Two other, smaller stone coffins. The Rabbi's wife and child. What a mess!

I suggested to Abdullah that if they cleaned the place up and made something of it, it could be a good basis for a key into Jewish tourism, and they certainly needed that. He said: 'I keep complaining to the municipality and they send somebody in and clean it up and then two days later, the youngsters are back there at night. They smoke and throw away their cigarette ends and bits and pieces.'

I suggested that they might put a gate across the entrance, to keep out the youngsters. He said: 'It's all a question of budget.' In Sakhnin, it always is. Private houses well kept, groomed, cleaned. Very little green – gardens a rarity. Homes smart. Houses proud. But anything communal has bottom priority. What a shame. But, as they say, '*khalas*' – oh well.

Back to the car and home and I go for a stroll up the hill and this time turn right, to a supermarket I have not been in. A group outside – I presumed they were the owner and family. They said: '*Ahlain*'. Welcome. '*Shalom*'. Well, they know everybody here and I am a stranger, and they rightly presumed that I was Jewish.

I bought a batch of ice-creams for my Shadi family to put into the deep freeze on top of the refrigerator in the living room in the guest house, plus a cone for me. I paid, and watched a woman spreading a plastic bag on a stack of plastic glasses. She poured some sparkling orange juice into the top glass. '*Tefadel*' – please have some, she said. I thanked her and took it and wondered where else in the world the proprietor of a supermarket would give you a free glass of drink, when there was no chance of your coming back and it was just done out of hospitality. I smiled and said: '*Ahlain*' and '*Shukran*' to the family group and headed home, eating my vanilla and chocolate cone.

Then to bed. I hope that Zoom the mosquito will not come back.

I thought of the book by my parliamentary colleague, Gerald Kaufman. He wrote that Israel's Jews live in their own bubble. They block off from their minds and from their lives the problems and perils facing fellow citizens and get on with their daily routines. That way, they keep reasonably sane and contented.

Israel's Arab Sakhninis do the same. They live in a mainly Muslim bubble, cosseted by the *hamoula* and largely governed by their own municipality which is underfinanced by a central government which otherwise and in the main leaves it alone to create its own political potholes. Within the bubble, these Arab citizens create and inhabit their own Arab environment. Within it, they are secure. Within it, they have their own joys and sorrows, qualms and quarrels. And within it, they have made me – their Jewish visitor – vastly welcome. Apart from some ancient Jewish guests who arrived at Abdullah's elevated bed and breakfast on my last day, and a few visitors from local Jewish settlements who came for the shopping – and apart from the newly arrived Jewish wedding photographer from Kiev – I met no other live Jews during my bubble bath. Rabbi Yehoshua of Sakhnin had been dead some 1600 years. His tomb and sarcophagus are the late night haunt of Sakhnin youngsters, who would like to break out of the bubble and cannot.

Another good day gone. *Khalas.*

Chapter Eleven

HOME AND ABOUT

L et me now describe my new and happy Arab home.
Bedroom: about ten foot square, with a modern, light-
coloured, wood headboard to the double bed, and similar
wardrobe. An oil lamp on top – also a basketwork vase. Another
bed along the back wall and picture of a boy with geese – in three-
dimensional yellow, white and green. The picture could be
anywhere in the world. And so could the bathroom and shower,
neatly installed in the far corner.

Into the living room. Two other bedrooms lead off it. It's got
everything. Kitchen – stove, refrigerator, small white microwave.
And home-made olive oil, for sale.

The main part of the room: about fifteen foot by eight. Chairs
and couches in basketwork on either side. And Arab pictures on
the walls. Men on donkeys. Women with pitchers on their heads,
and Hebrew posters, alongside. A gold framed, shiny picture with
two white doves and 'PEACE, SHALOM & SALAAM', in

The Halayle family outside their home: (back row, left to right) Jowdat, Abdullah, Fawzieh; (front row, left to right) Shadi, Jihen, Asmahan.

The garden of the guest house.

English, Hebrew and Arabic – and an inscription in Hebrew addressed to 'Our dear friend, Abdullah Halayle – 1996,' wishing him luck with the Shadi Guest House, from someone called Omar Drusha.

Double doors, glassed, and with curtains pinched in at the top, leading onto the patio. Alongside, a permanently lit blue anti-mosquito lamp. On the right of the door, a painting of an Arab man leaning against an olive tree, with a lad at his feet and a hill town in the distance. Below it, a shelf with a payphone.

To the left, a hand-made, wicker basket – and alongside it a fire extinguisher. A blend of old and new, at the same time homely and relaxed.

On the table in the middle, a book for guests to sign, filled with Hebrew inscriptions, from grateful guests. If everyone is so happy, why is the place so empty? Answer: because Sakhnin has no tourist initiative and people do not realize how happy they could be in the Shadi Guest House. And too many Israeli Jews are scared of staying in an Arab home or hotel.

Outside there is the patio. The gnarled olive trees on either side, with their birdcages and hanging gongs. A small circle of green around the far edge, inside the green fence. About the only grass in town. And the light white cement patio with half a dozen tables and chairs. That is where we eat. That is where I am sitting now. Alongside an octagonal, six-inch-high container with half a dozen different ancient coffee pots in it. Bronze-coloured. Folk lore. And on the grass, the green and white umbrellas, with another gnarled olive tree and a cage with one yellow, chirpy canary bird.

Breakfast arrives. Today, it is hummous. A plate full, with a pool of oil and chickpeas in a central pile. Enough food for an army. Salads – cucumbers, tomatoes, cheeses and sour cream. Home-made orange juice – Jowdat tells me that he made it for me, himself. And coffee, with hot milk. *Walima* – a feast. *Lathith* – delicious.

I yet again show Jowdat the paddle trick. Relax. Magic is the art of trickery.

I recalled the greatest compliment of my magical career. David Berglas – then radio and TV's man of magic, my friend, and a great President of the Magic Circle – gave me some lessons. He got quite irritated by my clumsiness and finally told me my problem, quietly and ominously. 'Greville,' he said, 'magic is the art of deception. Your trouble is that you are too honest!' Words of unparalleled rarity, for any politician . . .

I show Jowdat how to make a knife look as if you have broken it, when you have not. And how to levitate it, with your hands. Much laughter.

Abdullah has gone to school to correct exam papers. Jowdat will take me to the bank.

Fawzieh comes by. Anything else? Have you had enough to eat? *Shukran, kafaya keda.* More than enough. Enough for an army. But then I do not know the word 'army' in Arabic . . .

After breakfast, Jowdat took charge of me. We drove first down the hill to the bank.

Driving in Sakhnin is an art. Its purpose: to avoid hitting people or cars or buildings – or potholes or pavements – when there are any, which is not often and usually they crop up when there should not be any, just to keep you on your toes.

I have come to the conclusion that it is all designed to remind people what it was like when you drove a donkey. Nice and slow. Gentle. Give way – *tefadal.* Wave your thanks when others wait for you. Do not rush. Be patient.

We edged our way down the roads, through the children, past the cars and the occasional tractor, to the Mercantile Bank. I had phoned Arik's Solomonic police chief saying that I would like a few words with him. He said, come back whenever you like. We agreed on 11.00. He was only five minutes away.

I parked the car where a pavement should have been but was not, next door to a car that should not have been there but was, and went into the bank. It was twenty to eleven. Plenty of time. I left Jowdat, sitting on the step of the building beside the car. He will keep an eye on it.

The bank is modern, air-conditioned, quiet, with the usual corridors of ropes to guide your way. 'Please wait here' – in Arabic, Hebrew and English.

I asked the clerk where I could change foreign money. He pointed to a man who signalled me to sit down. I produced 75 pounds sterling and 70 US dollars. He rejected a 20 dollar bill because it had a slight tear in it, but took the rest.

Then he took my passport, my Visa card and the money, to the head of the bank in his private office at the back, who eventually gave his authority for the exchange, on the basis that I had a daughter in Jerusalem (whose address he took) and that I was staying with Abdullah (whom everybody knew).

The clerk then filled in two forms in triplicate, stamping each and I signed each and this took ten minutes.

Back he went to the boss, to authorize the transaction. The manager was on the phone, chatting and laughing, and soon I strolled over and asked them very politely whether they would be kind enough please to get on with it because I had to meet the chief of police at Misgav in five minutes and I was going crazy, not that it mattered to them.

I reminded myself of the wise Arab admonition: Allah is on the side of the patient. By nature and in spite of all my legal training, patient I am not. I would be immensely grateful, I told them, if they would be kind enough please to hurry. They laughed at my Arabic and at my rush but they did not put a thumb and two fingers together as a Jewish bank person would certainly have done, and they said '*ayah khedma*' – which means, 'at your service', which they were.

The boss gave his consent and we went back to the desk where, to my horror, the clerk fed the information into a computer. Why did he not do that in the first place? Because I could not sign a computer. Why could I not have signed the document which came out of the computer? Because that was simply the final document which does not take signatures.

So the document came out and he put it on his desk with a broad smile of satisfaction. He then pulled out his calculator and worked out how much money I was going to get for the dollars and the pounds – separately. Everything took twice as long because there were both pounds and dollars. I wish I had thought of it before and I would not have given both – in fact I would not have come at all.

Anyway, he finished his job, stood up – held out his hand and I shook it and said thank you and please can I have my money. 'Over there,' he said, pointing at the queue on the far side, where one bank clerk was looking after one person and another three people were in the queue.

By then, I was almost weeping and decided to go and see the boss again. Which I did. And I was successful, because Abdullah knew one of the bank clerks who knew me and who thought I was a member of the British Parliament and had told the boss, who was very honoured to keep me waiting, and not some ordinary mortal. He sent the bank clerk over to pay the money which, after much preparation, he did.

At about 11.15, after a half-hour of totally unnecessary bureaucratic misery, I emerged from the bank. I recognized once again that I am not a *saaber* – a patient person. But Jowdat is. He had dressed himself smartly in his khaki slacks, and was still sitting on the step of the shop, next to the car, guarding it jealously. No sign of any irritation. That's the way life is. I know from experience in Israeli banks in Jewish towns that Speedy Gonzales would not have a chance there either. But this bank is the ultimate.

Off we go to the Misgav police HQ. I press the button by the sliding, steel gates. They are expecting me. The great gates grind and slide open and in we go, Jowdat and I. Warm greetings from the man at the desk who remembers me from yesterday and into Efraim's room. Cakes, coffee – 'You *must* have some. You *must* drink.' I told him about the bank and apologized for being late and he laughed. 'It's because we haven't got a free currency yet,' he said. 'We'll get it in a year or two. *Inshallah*.'

I gave him a parliamentary pill-box. We chatted a little. He wanted to know what I had been up to and I told him and he said that he would be grateful if I would do something for him. He pulled out a badge for the Civil Defence Force and gave me one. He would like me to help him to introduce this idea into Britain, because if people who are on the borders of crime are brought in to do something active against it, it is a wonderful weapon. Do I know about it?

Indeed. Laura has just started as a member and is learning to shoot guns. But is this really such a brilliant way to teach people who are on the borders of crime not to commit it?

He reminded me that the older ones would have been in the army anyway, so what the hell. The younger ones will be in the army, so they might as well learn soon. And if you are on the side of authority, it does tip the balance and we should do it in Britain.

Well, we did during the war, didn't we? But I doubt whether even the Home Secretary, my friend Jack Straw, would greatly appreciate the advice at this stage. Still, let's have a go. I suggested that when he came to England, I would introduce him to the Chief Commissioner of the Metropolitan Police at the time, and he could try the idea out on him. You never know. Maybe there could be some version that might help. Why not?

We went outside and took three photographs. I took him on his own and then with Jowdat and then Jowdat took him and me.

Then back to town and to the Post Office. No problem here. The counter clerk had been at the *ors* – the wedding. We had a brief chat.

Now, I must tell you that whilst my Arabic is bearable and my English remains quite good, what impressed me most was that all my conversations with the chief of police were in Hebrew. And I was not mixing up Arabic and Hebrew as I thought I would. On the contrary – I can use a Hebrew word when I cannot get the Arabic one and most of the Arabs here understand what I say, which is a help. Pity it is not the same in other Arab lands.

★

I now know why Fawzieh did not clean the room. The culture here is that you do not enter people's rooms without their permission and I had not given mine. I said to her this morning: 'Do you have a key to my room?' '*Nam*' – yes. 'Well, please do come in whenever you wish.' 'You'd like me to clean your room?' 'That would be very kind.' 'A pleasure. *Aya khedma* – at your service.'

So not only was the room cleaned today but she asked me whether I would like her to do my laundry and I certainly would. I only hope that she lets me pay for it. Which may be a problem because having changed the money at the bank I find I have not got enough. I phone Laura and David in Jerusalem and leave a message on the voice mail and would they please send a cheque for the guest house bill and I'll speak to Abdullah about it this evening.

Now, where do I buy some handkerchiefs? I say to Jowdat: 'I am sad that there is no *sooq* – no market – in Sakhnin. There are shops, but no *sooq*.'

'Today, there is a *sooq*. Until 1 o'clock,' he tells me.

So off we go in the Cavalier, to the *sooq*, at two miles an hour, avoiding children and potholes and cars and carts. Luckily, it's not a country village, so at least there are no animals. Yesterday, when I drove to Misgav, I did manage to swipe down a dove and kill the poor creature and leave its feathers floating in the air, but that was on the main road and it was a wild dove and not a domestic creature and I was very sorry, but what could I do?

We wended and wound our way around and up and down and sideways until we reached the *sooq*. I left the car on a hillock under an olive tree and walked across the road to a stall – a table, with household items. Jowdat asked whether they had handkerchiefs and they produced a huge bag of paper ones. 'Too many,' I said.

The man behind the counter started shouting and yelling and waving his hands in the air. Jowdat shrugged: '*Hooa majnoon*.' 'He's mad,' he said, pointing at his head and turning his finger in the universal gesture of lunacy. We moved off, fast.

The *sooq* was in a derelict, unkempt field, with a collection of stalls. There was the fruit *sooq*, the clothes *sooq* and between them the bits-and-pieces *sooq*. We did not want food so we moved to a stall that sold men's and women's clothing and, *hawi samawi* – lo and behold – handkerchiefs. I bought six.

I needed a cap because I had not brought one and the sun was beating down on my head. Laura had told me to keep out of the sun and I must do what she tells me or otherwise I will be in trouble! Jowdat wanted me to buy a cap in the shape of a basketball but happily it was twice the cost of one that had LA on it – which was only ten shekels which is two pounds, so that is the one I bought. Very smart.

Back to the car and off towards home. I stopped at a shop that sold, among a variety of other essentials, plants. I bought four splendid ones, for Fawzieh and Abdullah, as a thank you.

When we arrived home, Jowdat leapt out of the car and yelled to his mother: 'He's just spent 100 shekels on plants for you!' I yelled at him: '*Ooskut* – shut up!' He was quite startled. I explained to him quietly that what I choose to buy for his parents was my business and not his and he must not tell them what it cost and just help me instead to bring the plants inside.

My hosts thanked me but protested that I was extremely wicked and should not buy them things and it was their pleasure and honour to have me in their home and I must stay as long as I like. Also, would I please tell Laura and David that they and the children should come as his guests and stay in his hotel and he has rooms available and they might as well be filled as empty and he would be honoured if they would do the filling? I told him in my best Arabic that they would be deeply honoured – but unfortunately, they have to work. There were more thanks when I produced a bag of ice-creams, which Jowdat and I had bought in our favourite supermarket up the road, run by the man who was at the wedding with us.

They wanted me to have lunch. 'Greevil, you must be hungry. You don't eat. You will starve. I am nervous,' said Abdullah, 'because you don't eat.' But by then I couldn't cope with anything other than going back to sleep. So I did, for an hour and a half. Then I put on one of the music tapes which I had bought at the supermarket for Douglas and for me, and slept some more.

When I woke, I contemplated the bargaining routine in the Sakhnin market which is much the same as everywhere in the Arab world. It is as much an intellectual enjoyment as a means of fixing the price. If you simply pay what they ask, then they accept your money with appreciation but dismiss you as a rich foreigner who does not know how to behave.

In one epic scene in *The Life of Brian*, Brian is fleeing from the Roman soldiers. He decides that his only hope is to disguise himself. He stops breathlessly at a vendor, who is selling false beards. 'How much is one of them?' he asks.

The vendor names a vast sum. 'Fine,' says Brian, 'I'll have it.'

'No, no,' says the vendor. 'That's only the first price. What is your last price?'

'I don't care what the price is. I'll buy it,' Brian cries out in agony, as the soldiers get closer.

'Sorry,' says the vendor, shaking his head. 'No negotiation, no sale.'

The noble art of negotiation involves patience. The vendor names the very top price that he thinks that you just might pay. You respond with the very lowest price that he just might take, without being offended. Then you go back and forth and eventually, if all is well, you come down somewhere in the middle. You shake hands with a big slap and put your right hand to your chest. The game is done. Honour is satisfied.

If there is no bargain, there should be no hard feelings. '*Khalas*' – never mind. '*Koon bekhair*' – be well. '*Illa al-liqa inshallah*' – see you again – God willing.

In general, the more major the purchase, the longer the negotiation. My LA cap took only about three minutes. But I spent over an hour in a small shop in a *sooq* in Casablanca, buying an array of brilliant dressing-up clothes for the grandchildren, to a massive total of some 30 pounds. Allah is with the patient, and if you are not prepared to be patient, go back home to North London's Brent Cross shopping mall.

Chapter Twelve

ABRAHAMIC BROTHERS

Why do I bother to learn Arabic? It is a challenge and certainly Sakhnin has helped lift my spirits, for the first time since Myra's death. But it is more than that. People are happy when you try to speak their language, even if you destroy its beauty.

As Efarim Solomon, the police chief, told me: 'It's respect. You respect other people by at least trying to talk their language. And it's a great mistake that we do not respect our Arab fellow citizens by teaching our Jewish children Arabic as their second language. Yes, it's fine to teach English. But that should come after our other national tongue, shouldn't it?'

I am sure he is right, but I am just fascinated by the difficulty of my task. It has taken years to reach even the most modest standard. At least most of the words that Douglas has taught me in his 50 tapes are starting to emerge in the right places. And each day starts with my lesson with Jowdat. Magic for him and Arabic for me and laughter for us both.

Today, I again try to teach Jowdat the paddle trick and he goes through the names of animals again, and my new words. An hour of exchange that is fine and fun.

Abdullah asked me whether it is true that I spoke to Shimon Peres yesterday. He 'couldn't help hearing' my end of a telephone call. Yes, it is.

And did Mr Peres phone me or did I phone him?

I phoned him.

A pity. I can see that it was not as good as he had hoped. It would have been much better if Peres had phoned me. But still. . .

'You sleep well?' he asked me, in English.

'*Nam* – yes – *shukran* – thank you,' I replied in Arabic and reminded him of his promise to talk Arabic to me.

'How else am I going to learn English if I do not use your services?'

Which is fair enough, I suppose. But it must stop or I will not learn.

We sit on the patio and I eat my morning salads and sour cream, with *khubs* – pitta type bread – and washed down with fresh, ice-cold orange juice and sweet coffee. Then the inevitable omelette. Ah well, why not? Don't I have the inevitable muesli, every morning at home? And do I complain about the monotony? I do not. I complain if I can't get it.

Abdullah goes off to work and I am on my own for a moment. Meditation: isn't it strange and wonderful that not one person – with the possible exception of a few hints dropped in by mayors and ex-mayors – has used my presence to press a sustained, political attack against Israel, or the Jewish people, nor still less, against me?

A policeman in reception at Misgav asked me: 'How is Tony Blair?' That is the nearest I've got to British politics. Of course, the complaints about land and budgets were no doubt fair enough. But it is ordinary conversation and everyday life and courtesies that count here. With Abdullah and his family and their *hamoula*. And the people I keep meeting in shops and on the street who saw me at the wedding and asked how I enjoyed it and chat about town and encouraged me with my Arabic and laugh when I do not pronounce it properly and wish me luck and '*ahalain*'.

No politics. Just pleasure. And apart from my police chief and Arik and the Ukranian photographer at the wedding, I have found no Jewish people here. I am doubtful even about the dead one, Rabbi Yehoshua of Sakhnin. I would be very sorry if his revered bones were in fact under that pile of rubble in his dark and cigarette-butt strewn sarcophagus.

This afternoon Harry Rose from the Abraham Fund picked me up to show me a project involving Arab and Jewish youngsters.

Harry is in charge of the local programme of the Shemesh organization. Its job – to bring together local Jews and Arabs. It does so through projects, groups, summer camps, a choir and courses, and works for 'coalition for co-existence'. It is supported amongst others by the Abraham Fund, whose creator and benefactor, Alan B. Slifka, came to see Douglas and me in London. An impressive, tall, middle-aged American philan-thropist, with a vision of peace between the descendants of Abraham, Father of both our peoples.

Harry drove me to Misgav, the town with the police station on its nearest edge. A middle-aged and ascetic-looking man with a black beard and great spirits, he speaks Hebrew with an American accent.

We arrived within ten minutes at the youth centre – a fine, modern building in which everything seemed to work except the chocolate-vending machine into which I put my three shekels. Happily, a young muscled youth won them back for me by giving the nasty object a good thumping.

That afternoon, a group of youngsters from local Arab and Jewish towns, villages and kibbutzim were to hold a mock election. Alas, it was school holiday time and the Jewish world was elsewhere. Only one Jewish lad, called Shlomo, arrived from a local kibbutz – but then he was the organizer and he told us that he had himself almost forgotten to arrive.

Disappointing. About ten Arab youths, boys and girls, aged between 15 and 18 – together with a very bright and handsome young Arab named Forsein, who is studying in the US, at Brandeis University, with a grant from the Abraham Fund.

The youngsters gathered and got their instructions from Shlomo and moved off into two groups, sitting on the lawns outside the building. Green, spiky, local grass that lives well in great heat and does not need too much water. I decided to talk to the leaders and learn as much as possible from them.

One of them was Amin Aburaye, the moustached, handsome and impressive Arab in his mid-forties whom I had met at the museum. He told me that in his opinion the reason why Sakhnin is so badly organized is that the new mayor has different priorities from his predecessor. He has appointed dozens of new employees at the municipality – too many, from his extended family.

'The roads were much better under the old mayor. Everything he did, the new mayor has destroyed.' I remembered my favourite definition of a statesman: 'a dead politician'. We are much admired, at our funeral.

I asked Harry and another American worker called Gary whether it is true that Arab towns received less money than Jewish ones. Yes, it is. The reason: discrimination – going back 50 years. But it is improving, in special ways – for instance, Arab pupils in schools now get the same allocation of money as Jewish pupils. The problem: that they are starting from a lower base.

Relations between Jews and Arabs in Sakhnin and nearby towns and settlements, like Misgav? Amin told me that seven or eight years ago, Jews were afraid to come to Sakhnin. Now they are there every day, shopping and using the bank facilities. But there is no social mix. Jews and Arabs work together, but they do not socialize. So they were not surprised when I told them that there were no other Jewish people at the wedding I attended. But if the groom had Jewish friends at work, he might have invited them.

I asked Gary how the Arab and Jewish youngsters at Shemesh

get on together. 'Fine,' he said. 'I have found that young people are the same all over the world. You know what a "JAP" is?'

'Of course. A "Jewish American Princess".'

Gary: 'Correct. You'd be surprised to know how many Jewish American Princesses we have amongst the Arab youngsters, especially in big towns like Sakhnin. Not so much from the smaller ones. They are more provincial and relaxed. But dealing with young people is the same all over the world and it doesn't matter if they are Jews or Arabs. They are not that much different. They are equally irritating.'

I pointed out to Amin the plaque at the entrance to the centre: 'The caring gift of Eve and Henry Rose, of California'. 'Haven't you got an Eve and Henry Rose somewhere in the world who could make a gesture to your town or work?'

'No, there is none. We have some wealthy Arabs in Akko and in Haifa but they prefer to give to their own communities.'

Both Harry and Amin confirmed that there is no tradition of local community giving, by local people for local causes. They build their comfortable homes and these usually take years to complete and they have their food and drink and there is nothing much left over. It is all priorities.

I asked Amin why his museum leaves everything open for people to touch and eventually to ruin. 'Budget,' he said. 'We need $36,000 to put everything into glass cases and we haven't got it.'

'Meanwhile, why don't you *ask* people not to touch? Why don't you put up signs?'

'I'm sick to death of trying,' he said. 'I've given up.'

I consoled him with the thought that in some ways this is the best museum I have ever been to because people feel part of it. Although it is very bad for the exhibits, it is excellent for the visitors. They can touch and feel and the objects belong to them and are not in another glass-encased world.

I asked Harry why there was so little contact between Sakhnin and the surrounding towns. 'It is psychology,' he said. 'They feel surrounded. OK, so it happened largely back in 1948, over 50 years ago. But the feeling is still there.'

'What are your main problems?'

'Bureaucracy. I have to get permits from the Israeli authorities, like for the summer camp. It is taking me a tremendous amount of time and effort and energy. They don't like my credentials. It is not enough that I have a Master's degree. If I were a head teacher, that would be fine. But here you need permission for everything from everyone and it's a pain.'

Meanwhile, Shlomo was moving back and forth between the groups and giving them their work. Each was to support a different political party and to vote for it and explain why and they would video it and play it back. They talked in a mixture of Arabic, English and Hebrew.

I said goodbye and how sorry I was that my Arabic was still not up to understanding what they said. 'Don't worry,' said Forsein. 'You are learning *fussha* – classical Arabic. We are talking local dialect.'

And that, I fear, I will never learn. *Abadan* – never.

Chapter Thirteen

DISSENT INTO HADES

It must be hell living in a country where you cannot dissent. At least for people like Abdullah and me, who like to follow our own paths.

Here is Abdullah, seeking a Jewish clientele for his Arab guest house. Not simply to make money, although they need it. The Halayles enjoy the company of people who are different – like me. For my part, he and his family are the breath of goodwill, precisely because they are Israeli Arabs, who are different. Vive la différence!

I salute the tradition of dissent which Britain and Israel hold in common.

In the British Parliament, dissent may not always be welcome, but it is as rightly inevitable as freedom itself. When Israel's then Prime Minister, Menachem Begin, correctly and bravely ordered the successful bombing of the Iraqi nuclear reactor, the news was greeted in the Commons with vast unpopularity. I thought he was absolutely right, and at Prime Minister's Question Time, I said so.

I was greeted with roars of rage. I heard one of my party's most unpleasant anti-Zionists, shouting behind me: 'Go back to the Knesset'. I could not make myself heard above the hubbub.

Speaker George Thomas (later Lord Tonypandy) rose to his feet, in wrath. 'Order, order,' he proclaimed. 'The Honourable Member is entitled to be heard.' And heard I was.

As I emerged from the chamber, a number of colleagues said, 'Well done.' They included several who disagreed with my words but who would go to the stake for my right to speak them.

In Israel, there are many outspoken advocates of Arab rights. Many of the best-known fighters for Arab equality are Jewish. There are over a dozen Arab members of the Knesset. They are spread across Labour, Meretz, the Front for Peace and Justice, the Arab Democratic Movement and even the Islamic Movement and a Nationalist Party called Balad.

British and Israeli laws both impose decent limits to freedom of speech. But those limits are themselves limited. For instance, you cannot lawfully publish certain pornography, or stir up race hatred. But the underlying approach is the basic right and freedom to speak your mind. Any restriction on that freedom must be justified, in the obvious interests of a free and honourable society.

The same does not apply in all Arab countries. There are those which I still cannot visit – Iraq, Libya and the Sudan, for instance. In others, you watch your words with a varying degree of care, if you wish to be a welcome guest, let alone a citizen at large.

Take Oman, where Douglas and I were received with cordial hospitality and made most welcome – a spectacular and kind people, worthy of the *Arabian Nights*. There is freedom of speech – provided that you criticize neither the ruler nor the Muslim religion.

In Syria, Douglas steered me away from a potentially virulent argument with students at the University of Damascus. Open argument and dissent may lead to trouble. Silence is too often golden.

Or take a nearby but non-Arab land – Iran. Life there was bad under the Shah, but it is not now the land of the free tongue. I think of my Iranian friend, Ayatollah Rouhani. He lives in exile in Paris but he recently stood for the Iranian Parliament. He reckons that he is the only candidate for any office in any country in the world who only received one vote – his own.

There is the classic tale of the occasion when President Truman welcomed to the United States the then Soviet leader, Josef Stalin. 'This is a country of mighty freedom,' he told his guest. 'Anyone here can say "to hell with President Truman" and nothing will happen to him.'

The Russian grunted. 'So what,' he said. 'Anyone in my country can say "to hell with President Truman" and nothing will happen to him either!'

In Israel, you can say: 'To hell with the Prime Minister', and nothing will happen to you, whether you are Arab or Jew. I once read a book called *Personal Freedoms in the Arab World – Cruelty and Silence* by Kana Makiya – a pen name, I was told. Was it too dangerous for the author to write under his own name?

The people of Sakhnin have real complaints, but they are free to complain, loudly and without fear. They are not sentenced to the shameful fate of silence. I am sure that if I lived in a country where it was a criminial offence to speak your mind, I would either spend my life in jail, or emigrate.

If you are an argumentative person in a society where you cannot speak your political mind in freedom, you do have some other outlets. There is business bargaining, for instance. I vastly enjoyed the full-throated, cursing haggling in Cairo's camel market, now moved down into the Delta. A serious process which may begin over sweet coffee in a huge tent and hopefully ends in the clapped clasping of satisfied hands.

Or you may argue with your wife or husband or partner or family. In every land, there is reason to be unhappy at home, and far too many make use of it.

I think of Myra. Of course, we had our arguments during those 42 years, but never over politics. She was more interested in personalities, in family and in friends and in the sensible values of home. She was my anchor. Held safely to the floor, I could float freely.

Within limits, though. Myra liked to have me at home, but not during the day. When I suggested retiring from the Commons, she said: 'That's fine, darling. Provided that you're out of the house by 8.30 in the morning.' But not in the evenings and at weekends. And she did not like being left at home, when I went on trips abroad.

Myra enjoyed overseas visits, provided that she was physically comfortable. 'What's the point,' she used to say, 'in going on holiday if you are less comfortable than you are at home?'

We enjoyed our journeys together to Jordan, to Egypt and especially to Morocco, where the great Mamouniya Hotel in Marrakesh provides facilities far better than even the most luxurious of homes.

We all accept limits on our freedom, then. Marriage means compromise. In my case, that meant at least some sensible limits on my freedom of movement. 'Fair dos,' as my Australian wife would put it. 'Fair crack of the whip.'

I wonder whether Myra would have enjoyed Sakhnin. Certainly the Halayles would have loved her.

Israel's then Ambassador to Britain, Moshe Raviv, asked me to chair the British celebrations for the 50th anniversary of the establishment of the State of Israel.

I asked myself: if I accept, how do I cope with my profound dislike of the politics of Israel's current government?

On my usual basis. I shall say: The trouble with democracies is that they keep electing people whom I would never vote for. After all, as a Member of Her Majesty's loyal Opposition for 18 years, I happily celebrated the greatness of Britain, whilst trying to get rid of its government.

The positive side is more important. Life for the world's small Jewish population was very different, before the creation of the

Jewish State. My generation remembers. I remember when the people in the Bergen Belsen Displaced Persons' Camp had nowhere in the world to go, nowhere that wanted them, nowhere that opened its arms to receive them. To our shame, the Britain of Balfour was led by the government of Bevin. The gates to Palestine were sealed.

Yes, 1948 was indeed a great year in the lives of our people. I accepted the role of chairman.

I asked the Israel Embassy to let me have their draft for the objectives of the anniversary year. I received a list, which included: 'To celebrate the State of Israel in all its aspects.'

'In all its aspects?' No. I would not celebrate our own British society 'in all its aspects'. Were we now to celebrate the fact that after 50 years, Israel's Arab and Jewish communities live so firmly apart – and not always in equality? Or the narrowness of the ultra-orthodox and of the other extremists of the Jewish State?

No. We will celebrate the massive miracle of the existence of Israel . . . its democracy, with all its faults, a brilliant contrast to military or dictatorial rule, where dissent is so often beaten down and crushed.

Yes, Arab Israel has many legitimate complaints. But it is free to complain.

Maybe in another ten years, we shall be able to celebrate Israelis, Arab and Jewish, living together in peace and security, from without and within. *Inshallah*. God willing.

Chapter Fourteen

ABDULLAH AND
FAWZIEH

*A*l *hamdulillah!* God be praised – more guests have arrived.
Seven of them. This means, though, that I must move out of
my palatial, three-bed suite, alongside another room with another
three beds in it. I am off to Room Five.

It has a double bed and a single, brown wooden wardrobe, and a
TV. But no obvious outlet from the living room air-conditioner.
And only one window, so no cross-breeze.

Three tiny wooden carpeted steps lead up to the shower and
loo, past a brown wood-encased basin.

A refrigerator in the corner, a little table with two white chairs.
And the same bed lamp – that's good. This guest house is one of
the few places which is light, bright and convenient, for pre-sleep
reading.

I pile everything into my bags, all except the bottle of water and
the stamped postcards and the camera and portable telephone.
Check – nothing left behind. Passport. Ticket. And, as usual,

when I am checking, I think of my old friend and mentor, Davide Sala, and his joke about the Jewish man who saw his friend crossing himself before he left home. 'Why are you doing that?' he asked, shocked. 'Why should a Jew make the sign of the cross?'

'It isn't the cross,' his friend replied. 'It's spectacles, testicles, wallet and watch.'

Anyway, Abdullah helps me take my non-bodily possessions across and install myself, shirts and all, in my new, one-night home. He climbs on a chair and pushes open a vent at the top of the wall, and cool air rushes in.

Fawzieh had washed my shirts, as she promised. I bet they won't let me pay for that either. What a b&b.

Breakfast: hard-boiled eggs this time, with marvellous salads, home-squeezed orange juice, ice-cold, and sweet coffee, of course. Abdullah asks what shall we do today and we decide that we will travel around in the morning together. Then I go off to Gan Ner – the village named after my family – in the afternoon. In the evening, Jamal has invited me to dinner in a restaurant.

Abdullah shakes his head in disbelief. 'No,' he says. 'You will have dinner here.'

I explain that Jamal is already *za'alan* – cross with me – upset. I had promised that he would teach me Arabic and it had never happened. Now was the time to spend a little time together. Secretly, I was looking forward to my first good talk in English, to try to get below the surface a little in a way that you cannot do in the elementary and almost childish beginners' words in a new language.

While Abdullah and I are enjoying our breakfast, I notice the sound of the loudspeaker. Across the hillside comes a voice with words I cannot understand. 'What's that?' I ask.

'The muezzin. Someone has died. They are inviting people to the funeral. At 3 o'clock. We bury people very quickly here.'

'Like the Jews.'

I think of asking to go to the funeral so that I will have a glimpse of another side of Arab life – death. But no. Privacy for the mourners – and survival for me. I realize that I had not written a word for any book since Myra died. In the last five days, I have written twenty thousand. If I go to the funeral, it may crack the illusion and bury my creativity along with the desceased Sakhnini.

Abdullah: 'So we leave for Dir Hana?'

My police chief had said that I should see it. Like Kawkab. Well run and clean. No rubbish lying around like in Sakhnin and Arraba.

'*Nam.* Yes. Thank you.'

This time, I insisted on our travelling in my car. Jowdat climbed in the back, Abdullah in to the front seat and we were off.

Dir Hana is a clean, neat town, like Kaukab. The streets are organized and most of them are clean and well maintained.

Decent, clean, white stone-clad houses, like most of those everywhere in this area. Some trees, but little grass. A dusty football ground and a basketball field.

Then to Arraba, where we had been last night. Back to the higgledy-piggledy potholes, to the waste-strewn ground, even to a telegraph pole in the middle of a turning. I drove like the classic snail. In and out and up.

An Arab in a traditional white *kafieh* head-dress was carrying a long pole on his head. A woman followed behind, in traditional robes. Green. Her head covered – and topped by a basket. Could have been 2000 years ago. Abdullah said: 'Take photo?' But there was a car behind me and another ahead and I inscribed the picture in my mind instead.

Most curious: as if there were not enough potholes and hazards in the road already – enough, I thought, to halt a line of light tanks – most of the roads also have 'sleeping policemen' – man-made humps. So you drive slowly up a hump made by man and you land in a hole made by vehicles. You drive around the hole and stop dead in your tracks. A child runs across the road. Another car comes straight at you. A bus emerges from the side. A tractor tries to get by. A car hoots. I just sit. I turn on the tape, of Douglas, to show my hosts how I started learning my Arabic.

It was another day of cloudless susnhine, so we pulled up for the inevitable ice-cream and had the inevitable fight as to who was going to pay, but today was mine. They were my guests. They would have to put up with it, which they did with good grace and we ate our ice-creams and headed up the hill.

We reached the top of the mountain and curled our way down on a magnificent, snaking, two-lane, smooth highway, overlooking the whole of the Jordan Valley. We could see Galilee through the hills in the distance and the canal at the bottom. 'Eshkol built that when he was Prime Minister,' said Abdullah. 'It brings the water from Galilee to the Negev. Let's go down there, to the canal.'

Through olive groves and Arab villages, and trying to keep my eyes on the road when I wanted them to move across the valley, I watched the sun dappling the fields. Mercifully, the weather was cooler than at the weekend. The air-conditioning worked. It was an extraordinary drive.

We reached the canal and admired the cool, clear channel, bringing life to deserts. Then I turned round and drove back up. Lads on their bicycles pulled to the side and waved. The car wants to pass? '*Tefadal*' – help yourself. The cyclists wave again and so do I.

Up and up and then on to another road and past a kibbutz called Yahad. I drove in and around the small settlement. A line of identical homes, with that fabled view across the valley, but not a visible soul.

On, until gates closed and the road, with the universal STOP sign on it. Jowdat climbed out of the car and opened the gates and we drove through. It was a settlement called, in Hebrew, Hararit – the mountain top. Adbdullah knew the man in charge so we stopped outside the village office and the man said hello and welcome and then got back to his work as quickly as he decently could.

I suggested that we had some tea but Abdullah said: 'No, we'll park outside the tea house and then I've something to show you.' I did and we ambled in the sunshine across a ploughed field. It was now blazing hot. I put knots in the corners of my handkerchief and attached it to my head. I did my best to avoid the thistles, especially the startling, light mauve variety. And I wondered why we could not look at the valley view from the village. Why did we have to climb over rocks in the heat? Then I found out why.

We came to a line of brown, stone steps. Simple and hand-made. Up we climbed.

At the top, a sign in English, Arabic and Hebrew: 'Welcome to the chapel. Please come in but remember that this is a place of prayer. No food, no smoking, no talking.'

Abdullah did his brave best to explain in Arabic-English that we had come to a monstery. We passed two shacks. A man was sitting reading on the veranda of one of them and carefully took no notice of us. Round the corner, the chapel.

Local brown stone and with a cross at the top. I stopped and asked Abdullah to be silent for a moment. The voice of the muezzin was loudspeakering across the hills. Allah is Great. There is only one God and it is time to come and pray to him. Silence. Abdullah talked. No, Abdullah, please. Let's just be still for a moment.

Suddenly, the small bell at the top of the chapel clanged. Clang, clang, clang, clang.

We walked to the door. It opened. An elderly man with a thin, Semitic face and a white beard was smiling at us. He held a key in one hand. He was wearing a black skull cap. 'Are you Jewish?' I asked, astonished.

'No. We are Greek Orthodox. I am Father Jacob. Welcome.'

'Thank you. Have you been here for long?'

'Thirty years.'

'Are there many of you?'

'Four. And one applicant.'

'Please may we come in?' I had seen that inside and past the small chapel on our left were some stairs – brown stone, leading down, and with a monk with long hair, black and pulled into a ponytail, sitting on one of them.

'Sorry. It's prayer now. For the next 15 to 20 minutes.'

He signalled us to leave and smiled and bowed.

'*Ephkharisto*,' I said in my best Greek. Thank you.

'*Parakalo*,' he replied. 'You are welcome.' Then he pulled the door closed and locked it and we walked back by a better route to the tea house.

A woman greeted us on the veranda and carefully closed the door behind her as she went into her house. Yes, there are *sherutim* – toilets. You go in through the outside and not through her house.

We drank orange juice and Coca-Cola and then chatted with her husband – a tall, smiling man with black shorts and a T-shirt. He is an electronics engineer and works as a consultant to all the surrounding factories. It's a good life and they are doing fine, thank you.

Abdullah talked to the woman, in Hebrew. They discussed trade. It's been OK but not good at the moment. Unemployment. The economy not doing very well. It hits tourism. 'It's up and down, like these hills,' said the woman, making sweeping gestures with her left hand. '*Yiheyeh tov*' – it will be OK.

Many thank-you's and '*toda*', then back to the car and a short cut through Arraba. Well, the road was short but the time was not because we stopped and started and jiggled and wiggled our way back to the main road. Turn right. Straight on. Up past the bank and up the hill and down that narrow, incredibly steep slope that leads to the guest house.

'Jibril' – that's Greville or Gavriel in Arabic and they called me that because it's easier. 'Jibril,' said Abdullah. 'It's time to eat.'

'Sorry, I can't,' I said.

'You don't eat much, do you? But you must have lunch. Fawzieh is expecting you.'

'Sorry. I must sleep. I can't eat. But a glass of orange juice would be lovely.' Which they brought and I thankfully drank and then went to my new room and out like a light.

Half an hour later the phone rang. It was Myra's brother, Jonathan, from Jerusalem. Would I not come back a bit early on Friday, tomorrow, so as to have lunch with him and with some Australians. Rabbi Lubovsky.

Now, I love my brother-in-law and his family, but the idea of missing even three hours of this place was just not acceptable.

'Sorry. I'm leaving at two.'

'Can't you leave earlier?'

'Sorry, I promised Laura to be back at five and it takes three hours.'

'Oh, I thought it was only an hour.'

Which showed how often people visit Sakhnin. Still, it was kind of him to ask and he was pleased when I told him that for the first time since Myra's death, I was not only thoroughly enjoying myself for days at a time, but able to write. This diary is the first record . . . the first creative, non-business writing that I have been able to manage since Myra passed away. Which was nearly seven months ago.

Jonathan said: 'Perhaps this visit will crack the problem a bit.'

Yes, I hoped so. I suggested that he should come to Sakhnin and try it for himself. He laughed.

Ah well . . .

Chapter Fifteen

BEREAVEMENT

When I heard the muezzin, crying out the name of the dead, I thought of Myra. I must be honest, if only with myself. Sakhnin is not simply a place where I can learn to understand another civilization, and improve my Arabic. It is also part of the post–Myra healing process.

I suppose that all humans handle bereavement in their own way. Some cope through religious belief. Their beloved partner is in heaven and they will meet again. Well, as my dear friend, Rabbi Hugo Gryn, said shortly before he himself died: 'I don't believe it, but I would be happy to be proved wrong.'

For me, healing means: sharing, running and hoping.

Sharing my pain, with my family and very closest friends. It helps to talk. And as my cousin and oldest friend, Edmund Cohen – who not long ago lost his wife from the same dread disease – told me: I am lucky that I can cry. So I talk about Myra. Most of the time I am coping. And then something totally inconsequential and unimportant happens and I am down the emotional drain again.

Like the escalators at Heathrow Airport on my way to Israel. Myra was afraid of escalators. She would sometimes go up one, but never down.

Or getting off the plane at Ben Gurion Airport. Myra was afraid of the steep steps. Fear of the inevitable descent in Israel spoiled her journeys to Tel Aviv.

Or a shop selling handbags. Myra loved handbags and joyfully accumulated them by the elegant dozen. If I see a bag shop, I churn up.

But running is my key to self-control. I run from home, early in the morning, and do not get back until late at night. All day, I am on the move, except for my post-lunch nap. And as much and as often as possible, I am away – abroad and in places and circumstances that I did not share with Myra. Like Sakhnin.

I could not manage without my children. Daniel phones, several times a day, 'just to check up on you!' Marion has taken over some of Myra's role in keeping me disciplined. And she takes me away on those stressful anniversaries – those occasions that Myra and I celebrated together and which mattered so much to us both – her birthday, my birthday, our wedding anniversary.

I must keep fit, of course. Laura chides me about my level of cholesterol and tells me that she has only got one parent left and I must look after myself.

Finally, there is hope. Not of another wife. At least as I feel at present, that will not happen. I do wish that kindly, well-meaning friends would not invite me to dinner and sit me next to a widow or divorcee whom I do not know but with whom they hope that I might form a liaison. Myra's speciality was the 'shidduch' – the traditional and worthy work of the marriage broker. But I am not in the market.

In Sakhnin there is no danger from that side. I remember in 1950, when I was in Nazareth with my sister, Ruth. An Arab man offered me two camels for her – which Ruth and I agreed was not nearly enough. No one in Sakhnin has offered anything for me.

So what am I hoping for, as I wander through Sakhnin's streets and alleyways, nodding and smiling at my friendly hosts? The House of Lords. I would love to be there. Back in the rough and tumble and comradeship of Parliament, but with no elections. A place to serve and a platform for service. A great club. Interesting people. A good place to entertain and to be entertained. I do not cook and I do not want to be at home. It would make a big difference to my life.

No, I am not moving house. I am content in our home and those who know about bereavement tell me that you cannot chase away those haunting shadows by moving to another and unfamiliar place. So I am staying. But to be back in what is after all my second home, in Westminster, would be marvellous.

Shortly before my mother died, I drove her into Palace Yard and along the road that runs through and under the buildings of the Commons and the Lords and out through Chancellor's Gate. 'This has been my second home for half a century,' she said. I know what she meant.

Not long before she died, Myra said: 'Don't count on it, darling.' I have not . . . I shall not – but I do. It is Tony Blair's decision.

I think of Blair, now leading Britain. Why is he doing so well? Because he gives an impression of intimacy. People are fond of him. And of Cherie, his wife.

It was the May morning of the Blairs' triumph. They and we and New Labour had won the election, by a vast majority. We celebrated at that huge party in the Royal Festival Hall. Then the Blairs helicoptered down and Tony talked to us.

Outside the Hall, Marion and I were at the front of the crowd, behind the crush barrier. When Tony finished his triumphal speech, he and Cherie came down from the rostrum and walked along the crowd, shaking hands. Cherie spotted us and put her arms around me and said: 'How I wish that Myra were here tonight.' I wanted to cry. What a woman – at that moment, that unique moment, to think of Myra. And to remember her name.

Wonderful people.

So here I am in Sakhnin, hoping that it will help the wounds to heal. Running. And coping and hoping. A week before she died, Myra said to me: 'You *will* mourn for me, darling, when I'm gone, won't you?' I replied: 'Of course I will. But you're not going. When I go, you'll have to mourn for me.' Neither of us believed it. In Sakhnin, I am mourning for her.

Kind people have said to me: 'It was a merciful release, wasn't it? She's out of pain.'

It was not like that. In her last days, Myra pleaded: 'Help me, darling.'

'What help do you want me to give you?' I asked.

'Help me to get well.'

'Fine. So you take this drink and we'll get you well.'

She did not want to go. I cope, I run, I hope – and I mourn, even in Sakhnin.

I have to learn to cope without Myra's presence but with her memory. It is already over half a year since her death, but the pain remains, intermittent but sharp. I am better off here in Sakhnin because there is little to remind me of our love. Then something happens – like the loudspeakered announcement of someone's death – and I am crushed again.

I wonder how survivors of the Holocaust cope. One Israeli survivor told me: 'We don't talk much about the Holocaust here. We have an odd attitude towards it. We block it out and try to live normal lives.'

It is not at all odd. I understand it very well. The bereaved do not want to reopen wounds.

There is one great little London organization called Chai Lifeline. The people who run it are symbols of hope because each has recovered from cancer. They helped both Myra and me to cope. Now they want me to chair a fund-raising dinner for them. Sorry. Not yet. I am not that brave. I do not want to dissolve into tears in public. That is what happens when you reopen wounds and they hurt too much.

Sakhnin helps heal because it is unreal. Here, the pain is less, because I am away and starting to be happy, sometimes for hours. Because it is neither Myra's world nor mine.

I hope that the family of the dead and swiftly buried Arab will cope. May Allah console them.

Chapter Sixteen

GAN NER

Rochelle Mass came to Sakhnin in a taxi, to collect me. She told me that she and her husband had moved to Gan Ner, but were only allowed in after they had gone to Haifa and submitted to psychometric and other examinations, at a cost to them of 700 shekels (about £120). You cannot just buy a home in Gan Ner. You have to be tested. Will you be a good neighbour? Will you be a good citizen? Will you contribute to the life of the community?

When they advertised in a local newspaper that there would be homes for sale in the settlement, they were flooded with requests. It is regarded in the area as a mark of good fortune and an honour to be allowed to be at home in Gan Ner. It is certainly an honourable mark of good fortune to be able to contribute towards the quality of life of that remarkable, scenic and friendly place.

We sat on plastic chairs, with drinks on a long plastic table. We looked out beyond the gathering of Gan Ner people – adults and children – across the ancient valley of Jezreel, to the Mountain of Gilboa, with its stories of David and Jonathan and Saul. The village of Gan Ner is growing fast. Today, we symbolically put in place the first foundation of the swimming pool and leisure centre.

Speeches, into a microphone. Brief ones. Motti Cohen, Secretary of the settlement, recalling what it was like 17 years ago, when Shimon Peres and my mother inaugurated the project. Today, 400 families. Soon, 500. One day, maybe 10,000. More people than in Sakhnin.

The present and former heads of the Area Council; the representative of the Jewish Agency; the Chairman of the Gan Ner Council – all thanked the builders, the contractors, the architects – and especially, the Janner family.

Motti called on me to speak. Instead of staying at the microphone by the table like the rest, I took the hand mike from Motti and walked up to the smiling and curious audience. Here is an approximate translation of what I hope I said in my best Hebrew:

'I'm delighted to be here, and in the name of all my family and our friends – well done. We have all been glad to contribute towards this swimming pool and leisure centre, which we hope will give extra quality to all your lives.

'I know that there is a legend that the Janner family is extremely wealthy. Unfortunately, we are not. We work for our living – and the contribution that you have received towards this project came from hundreds of people, each of whom wanted to help you, by honouring my parents. So my sister, Ruth – who would have loved to be here – and I have joined with all our family and friends, and like the building of the Temple, each of us placing one brick on the foundations of your project.

'It was kind of everyone to thank my family. I'm in Israel so that I can be with you today, but also to learn the Arabic language. I have already spent four days in the Arab town of Sakhnin. And I have learned the beautiful expression: "*La shukr allal wajib*" – it is not something for which you should give thanks – it is a *mitzva*, a commandment to be fulfilled. And we are all very happy to be part of your lives.

'Enough for the adults. Now let me talk to the children.'

I turned to a small boy at the front: 'What is your name?'

The boy: 'Omer.'

GJ: 'Why did your parents call you Omer?'

The boy: 'I don't know.'

GJ: 'Well, you should ask them. Maybe you were named after your grandfather or grandmother or perhaps they just liked the name. So why do you think that your town is called Gan Ner? I'll tell you the story.

'The man who talked about my father as a brave and veteran Zionist was right. Menachem Begin liked him, especially because my father produced proof that the Irgun gave a warning before they blew up the King David Hotel.

'So when my father died and my mother wanted a place in Israel named after him, I went to see Prime Minister Begin, who received me with great couresty. I told him the problem.

'"Sorry," he said, firmly. "We could name a street after him and possibly a district, but not a town. We do not name places after people any more. Anyway, what sort of Hebrew name is Janner?"

'I said: "Yes, Prime Minister, I do understand. But let's forget Janner. How about 'Gan Ner?'

'"Ah, Gan Ner!" said Begin. "What a good idea. Yes, let's do it." And he did. It took some time, because he first offered places beyond the Green Line – outside pre-1948 Israel. My mother was not having any of that.

'Then they offered the settlement that is now Gan Ner – where you live – of which we are all so proud. And that is why and how it got its name.

'So, my family and I are delighted that we can help you to build this pool and leisure centre. For all of you – but especially for your young people.

'There's not much to do in Gan Ner for the youth, is there?' I looked at a woman in a police officer uniform. 'What happens when youngsters have nothing to do? They get into trouble, don't they?' She nodded. 'Well, the pool will help keep them busy.

'My only regret? That my parents cannot be with us. They would have been so proud today.

'Proud of the way the settlement has grown. Proud of its future. And proud of your new project, which we hope will give great joy to you all – to the children – especially to the youth – and to all of the grown-ups too.

'Good luck! And may we always meet on *semakhot* – on happy occasions, like this one.'

Digging the first sod proved an unusual venture, as they had already carved the hole in the hillside into which they will soon plant the aluminium sections of the new pool. Instead, Motti produced a bucket of wet cement and each of us on the top table slapped a trowelful onto the ground. Photographs. For the historical record. One of the workers said to me: '*Mabruk*' – congratulations. I replied: '*Wallah yubarik fik*' – may Allah bless you. A ring of workers smiled. They were Arabs.

So were a tall, grey-bearded man and his wife, there with a little child – the designer and the architect of the project.

My mother's friend, Naomi Nevo, was resplendent in a large straw hat and smiling from brim to brim. Beside her was Rochelle Mass, who had succeeded her as the PR person of Gan Ner. I asked Rochelle: 'What contact is there with neighbouring Arab towns and villages?'

'Informally, plenty. And everyone on good terms. Formally – none. There should be.'

Indeed. Perhaps I can put Shemesh onto this one.

The tiny kindergarten children who had mimed songs to start the evening moving were pulling at their parents' hands. 'I want to go home.' 'I want my tea.' 'I'm hungry.' 'I'm thirsty.'

Motti presented me with a framed photograph of the new Gan Ner, to put alongside the old ones – and of the pool area. It includes a hall, with glass cases for Janner memorabilia. The hall will be used for talks, lectures, gatherings.

We toured Gan Ner, in Motti's car. The 'old' houses and the new ones – red-roofed, comfortably nestling into the hillsides. Metalled roads. Children's playgrounds, well equipped. Soon, they are building an elementary school. Soon, they will have a swimming pool.

The Elsie and Barnett Janner Trust is contributing $125,000. Where is the rest coming from?

Motti said: 'We're applying to the Lottery . . . We're applying to the Jewish Agency . . . We are all chipping in ourselves.'

I know, it is easier for them than it would be for Sakhnin. But if faith does move mountains, and if initiative and energy can plant such a thriving community on the side of a mountain – surely the people of Sakhnin could find some way to start building a swimming pool . . . a park . . . a club . . . somewhere, for their young people to enjoy? What a contrast, between Gan Ner and Sakhnin. Not one to be proud of.

Before the ceremony and after it, we sat in Motti's office. I was hungry and pleased to be back eating a soggy bread roll, stuffed with cheese and cucumber. I noticed a mauve, Gan Ner T-shirt hanging on the wall. I told Rochelle the story of my problem in paying Abdullah and that I did not want a repeat with her, please. But would she get me some T-shirts. She gave me the one off the wall. Then she drove me back to Sakhnin.

Chapter Seventeen

TERRORISM – AND PEACE

Yitzhak Rabin once told me: 'You make peace, with your enemies, not with your friends.' Then, when Myra and I were in Oslo for the Nobel Peace Prize presentation – to Peres, to him and to Arafat – I asked him what he thought of the Palestinian leader. He replied: 'Politicians must deal with realities. Unless Arafat is murdered, which God forbid, we shall have to deal with him for the next 15 years. There is no one else.'

For Tony Blair, it is the Sinn Fein leader, Gerry Adams you must meet, if you are to grasp a hope of peace. There is no one else. Nor can you meet him without shaking his hand.

I once led a Board of Deputies delegation to see the then Prime Minister, Margaret Thatcher. Than her, there was no more powerful excoriator of terrorism in the entire democratic world. Towards the end of our conversation, she said: 'I'm sorry, but I must go. I have a meeting with Archbishop Makarios.'

At that time, Britain treated the Cypriot priest as a terriorist agitator. 'But he is a terrorist, is he not?' I smiled at the great lady.

'My dear Greville,' she replied sternly, 'if you want to make peace, you have to deal with terrorists.'

Thatcher could have added that today's terrorist may be tomorrow's President or Prime Minister. And not just in Cyprus, either. As I had reminded my audience at the Gan Ner ceremony, the man who agreed to name a village in Israel after my parents was Menachem Begin.

So yesterday's terrorists are today's negotiating partners. . . Your terrorists are other people's freedom fighters. . . Where is the limit? Their targets. Whether or not you aim your bomb or bullets at soldiers, or at civilians — at men of war or at non-combatants — at women and children, in buses or markets.

I thought of India and the Gandhi family. Of Mrs Gandhi's blood on the pavement. Of Rajiv Gandhi's funeral, with Sonia in mourning and their son, Rahul, setting light to liquid ghi on his father's body.

The day before the funeral, Rajiv Gandhi was lying in state, his torn body covered in plain brown cloth, with only his feet showing.

I joined the queue of mourners, waiting to sign the condolence book. I turned. Yasser Arafat was immediately behind me. I gestured that he should go ahead. *'Tfadal,'* I said. After you. He shook his head. 'No, Sir. You go.' I did.

That was my first meeting with Arafat. I have had many since and have never had cause to doubt Rabin's judgement.

Curious, I thought, that it was Rabin who was murdered by a Jewish terrorist. I remember asking Sadat whether he was not concerned about being assassinated.

'Not at all,' he replied. 'Mubarak will carry on my work, if I die. And anyway, what do you want me to do, go around wearing armour plate?'

It was an Egyptian who killed Sadat. . . Indians who murdered both Indira and Rajiv Gandhi. . . an Israeli Jew who assassinated his own Prime Minister. . . An American who destroyed President

Kennedy. . . Beware of your own. . .

How many Arab embassies are there in London? Twenty-five? And one Israeli mission only. Then why is the Arab case so often not well presented? Largely, because some of their presenters do not create a relationship with their audience. Instead, they fly over the top. They do not recognize that the Israelis, too, have legitimate concerns. If we are to reach the peace that my friends in Sakhnin want and need as much as their Jewish fellow citizens, then each side must present its case to the other in a way that is both understandable and ultimately acceptable.

For many years, I have made a decent living by teaching mainly business people how best to present themselves, their wares and their services. I have also, discreetly and voluntarily, trained many of Britain's top Labour politicians.

First lesson: that to get people's backing you must win their liking. If they like you, then they will at least give your case a fair hearing. If they dislike you, then they might still use your services or accept your point of view, but you considerably reduce your chances.

Next, ask the four questions:

Who? Who are your audience?

What? What do they want?

Why? Why are you doing it? Knowing your audience and what they want, what is your message.

How? How will you get your message across?

Now, apply these questions to a presentation on the Middle East which you wish to make to (say) an influential British audience. The answer to 'who?' is – people active in British political life, with their own constituencies to satisfy. What they want is to promote the interests of Britain. Your message must be: it is in the interests of Britain that you retain friendship with – the State of Israel or the Palestinians or whomever.

Recognizing that, in the main, British politicians are fair-minded, you must present your case in a fair way. You are not the only ones who want peace.

Abdullah and his family want peace. They recognize that peace is not only desirable for them personally and for their business but deeply necessary for their Jewish neighbours and guests.

After I returned home from Sakhnin, I found two immediate examples of these realities.

At the Labour Party Conference in Brighton, I attended a meeting of the Labour Middle East Council. It was chaired by my old parliamentary colleague and friend, Ernie Ross — a doughty Arabist but a fair and sensible opponent with whom you can have a civilized debate and remain friends. He was flanked on one side by Afif Safieh, head of the Palestinian Authority's delegation to the UK and a man whom I have always liked. Indeed, he did me the honour of inviting me to attend the confirmation of his daughters, in the Roman Catholic Cathedral in Jerusalem — a warm, hospitable and memorable occasion. On his other side was the former mayor of a small town near Bethlehem, who spoke quietly of problems which he said the Israelis had created. He made no mention whatever of Israeli concerns.

At question time, I paid my respects to both Ernie and Afif and then asked our guest one simple question: what are your views about Hamas terrorism and the suicide bombers?

Now, if you had asked that question of Abdullah, I know that he would immediately have condemned terrorism on both sides and sought a way to a peaceful life. He would perhaps have explained the motivations of the bombers, but in the context of the search for peace.

Instead, the mayor exploded, almost literally. He brought the microphone towards his mouth and shouted into it. He denounced the Israelis as creating the circumstances in which the suicide bombers felt that they had to act as they did. Only towards the end of his denunciation did he announce that he was against terrorism. By that time, I doubt if anyone believed him. He was probably sincere, but that is not how he sounded. Once again, through overstatement and no apparent interest in balance, the

131

Palestinian case had been weakened.

Then I received an article, written by a man whose company I had enjoyed and whose views I had respected when I met him in his days as British Ambassador to Jordan – Peter Hinchcliffe. He now describes himself as 'an academic, teaching Middle East politics at the University of Edinburgh'.

Mr Hinchcliffe gives his views in an article in *The Jordan Times* (29 September 1997): 'Instinctively, in my experience, most people in the UK who take any interest in the Middle East (and there are many because of historic ties) are more sympathetic towards the Arabs than toward the Israelis. But sadly, by contrast, politicians and therefore governments, appear to incline the other way for much of the time.' Why? 'Simply because the Israeli lobby is more effective in the UK than the Arab one.'

As to British people being 'instinctively more sympathetic towards the Arabs', that used to be true of British officials who served in Palestine. I remember Moshe Shertok – later Prime Minister Moshe Sharett – visiting our home, in 1946. I was a lad of 18, about to begin my National Service in the British Army. But I knew, not least from many conversations in our Zionist home, that the Foreign Office and most of those who worked for it in those days, were pro-Arab. 'Why is this?' I asked the Jewish leader.

'It's all a question of presentation, my boy,' he said. 'When a British diplomat visits an Arab leader, he will entertain him to tea in his tent and ply him with tasty and exotic sweetmeats. This is followed by a display of glorious horsemanship. The guest is entranced and delighted.

'When our Jews entertain the same person, they invite him to tea at home – and show him the family photographs!'

An exaggeration, perhaps. But we have learned.

It is true that Margaret Thatcher, John Major and now Tony Blair are all great friends of Israel and of the Jewish people. This does not make them in any way enemies of the Arabs. They are proponents of peace and want both sides to work towards it. But they are aware that there are two sides and two interests which may conflict but which all must recognize.

I have accompanied delegations of British politicians on visits to Israel. Of course, the Israelis showed them the best sides of Israeli life. They asked our four questions: *Who* are these people and *what* will interest them? Then they got their message across by showing their visitors what they — the visitors — wanted. This always included an understanding of the Arab case. They saw Israel and its population, warts and all.

All politicans have their constituencies. As many of my Conservative friends learned to their cost at the last election, if you do not keep your constituents happy, they will get rid of you. The more authoritarian and the less democratic the regime, the less this rule applies. But even unelected and despotic rulers will one day meet a grim fate if they do not provide both bread and circuses for their people.

In 1981, about six months before his tragic assassination, President Anwar Sadat received my daughter Marion and myself in his house on the Nile. I asked him how it was that if he and Begin were so deeply embedded in starting the Peace Process, he had put out a statement only a few days before, attacking Begin's policy on a delicate issue.

'Mr Janner,' he said, 'you do not understand. My friend Menachem and I each recognize that we have our own constituencies which we must satisfy.'

The two great men were able to do business together in the quest for peace because they liked and understood each other. They could disagree without being disagreeable. They not only recognized that the other had a case but that each must put his case, for the benefit of his own constituency.

Shimon Peres is another of the world's great men — a visionary, an idealist, a thinker. Yes, the Arab suicide bombers blew away his election chances, but that was partly because too many in his own Jewish constituency felt that he did not do enough to keep them and their families secure and safe.

You need a balance in political life. On the other hand, if you do not recognize that your opponents have a case, then you can neither meet nor undermine it. Equally, unless you ensure that your own constituency accepts that you are a sufficient advocate of their interests, then you will be knocked out of the game by your own team.

Peres's constituents were, in my view, totally wrong. It was in their interests to keep him at the head of their country, and his opponents far away from power. Only through peace can you achieve understanding and only through understanding is peace possible. But democratic electorates like the Israelis look at the realities of their daily lives. One of these was the fanatical, self-mutilating hatred of the suicide bombers. Because Peres had failed to eliminate them, his constituents threw him out of office. Which, of course, brought no end to violence.

A London man once went to the Law Society and asked to be recommended to a one-armed solicitor. 'Why one-armed?' asked the official. 'Because,' the man replied, 'I am sick to death of lawyers saying: "On the one hand this . . . and on the other hand that. . ."!'

On the one hand, if you do not recognize that others have a case, you will lose yours. On the other hand, if you do not put your case firmly, then you will not be an advocate for long. And without any hands, you certainly cannot clap.

It is all a question of balance. In their own quiet and dignified way, that is what my Sakhnini hosts had found.

There is nothing that I want for Israel more than peace with security. Under the leadership of Rabin and Peres, there had been peace but not enough security. Were it not for the suicide bombers, Peres would have been elected and the Middle East Peace Process would have moved forward. But now (I pondered) there is neither peace nor security. No one listens enough.

What a pity that Abdullah cannot host the next Peace Conference at the Shadi Guest House. Meanwhile, how sad it is that so few Jewish Israelis venture out of their bubbles into the world of Sakhnin. And that so few leaders on the stage of world politics and diplomacy recognize in public that the other side has a case.

The Sakhnin I encountered is a peaceful place. Shalom . . . salaam . . . the word is the same in both Hebrew and Arabic and that is what Arabs and Jews wish each other. Warm greetings – peace be unto you.

In both languages, they use 'peace' far more than we do in English. For instance, we say: 'Remember me to your wife.' In Arabic and in Hebrew, the equivalent is: 'Wish peace from me . . .' What I wish is peace for us and them. No more Jewish assassins like the maniac who murdered Rabin. No more suicide bombers, who believe that by sending Jews to hell, they will reach heaven.

Negotiation and not terror. Or as Prime Minister James (now Lord) Callaghan put it, 'Jaw, jaw, not war, war.' Sanity, not insanity. Life, not death.

Arab and Jewish Israelis share this fabled land. Sharing means communicating, understanding, seeking peace and working on common ground. The alternative is ill-will and division and misunderstanding.

For the Jewish people, the Jewish State is a prime historical necessity. It is as useless for Arab citizens to look back and say: 'It's all the fault of the Jews. . . If they weren't here, we would still have all our lands. . .', as it is for Israeli Jews to wish that problems caused by an Arab minority would vanish in a puff of magical smoke, or to imagine that territorial expansion is the key to security.

Yet the communities are separated, almost by mutual consent. Neither wishes to live in the lap of the other. Each has its own bubble. And each loses as a result.

On his way to Oslo, to sign the famous agreement, Shimon Peres stopped in Iceland's capital, Reykjavik. It was a bleak day. Iceland's Prime Minister told him: 'Well, you Jews may be the *chosen* people, but we are the *frozen* people!'

Many believe that God chose the Jews to suffer and the Icelanders to freeze. But (I thought to myself), Israeli Arabs and Jews should choose to know each other. Their relationship is too often too cool simply because of mutual ignorance.

There are seeds of goodwill, which we should water. Like a three-old-year Israeli Arab girl receiving the heart of an eight-year-old Jewish boy, killed in a road accident. The mothers met: The boy's mother said: 'Your daughter has received an angel's heart'. The girl's mother replied through tears: 'I know it's hard for you. But I do thank you.'

I wonder how a transplant of Israeli Jews to Sakhnin would work? Would they understand, for instance, the Sakhninis' feeling for their land?

We Jews should understand better than anyone else that eternal and atavistic craving for land. For 2000 years, we had prayed unsuccessfully and without cease for our return to Jerusalem, to the Land of our Forefathers. Now we have arrived, we must respect our neighbours.

We know in the Jewish Diaspora that when governments persecute the Jews today, tomorrow it will be other minorities – Catholics, gays, trade unionists, Quakers... Conversely, we British Jews live in a land where we are free – free to practise our own religion in all its individuality, and free, privileged and happy to serve others as well as our own community.

So why does the Jewish majority in Israel not comfortably absorb its Arab minority? Because they are perceived as a threat. Because they neither know nor understand each other. Because the message of Ibn Maimun has not got through to either side.

Oh, that I could wave my magic wand and produce peace in this land. The Holy One Blessed be He said: 'Let there be light' – light there was. Please would He come back and say: 'Let there be peace. . .'

Douglas taught me an Arab family proverb. Roughly translated it is: 'I and my brother against our cousin; I and my cousin against the stranger.' Fine. We all need the protection of our brothers and our cousins. But as my grandfather used to say, encouraging us to visit often: 'Don't make yourself a stranger'. If the Children of Abraham made themselves less of strangers to each other, then they would exchange the terror of war for the warmth of brotherhood. We are, after all, cousins.

Chapter Eighteen

SUPPER IN TOWN

Jamal – my would-be teacher of Arabic – collected me from my Shadi Guest House at about eight. We walked down the hill and he asked me what sort of food I liked. Anything Arab, I said. He suggested pizza. I said: 'No thank you. That's Italian.'

'Do you like felafel?'

'Yes.'

'OK, so let's choose one of these places around here.'

About four undistinguished and ordinary-looking cafés were spread around a small, squashed oval.

'Which do you prefer?' Jamal asked.

'Whichever is clean,' I said.

'They're all clean,' said Jamal. So he chose one and we stood at the counter and I took felafel and helped myself to a variety of salads, to fill up the pocket in the pitta bread. He chose kebabs. Then we sat on plastic chairs by a plastic table and chatted.

It took about two minutes before Jamal told me what he really wanted. He is a teacher and would like to go to England on an exchange. Can I help to get him on to some teachers' visit?

I told him that as I am no longer an MP, I have not got much influence, but I do know the British Ambassador and would gladly ask him.

'When will you let me know what he says?'

'No promises. I don't know what he'll say. He'll probably put me on to the British Council and I certainly will ask them.'

'Do Arabs get the same treatment as Jews at the British Council?'

'I'm sure they do. My guess, knowing the Council, is that Arabs get preferential treatment.'

'Why?'

'Well, in Jerusalem, the British Consul is concerned with Arab affairs and I'm sure that he has an input.'

'That's Jerusalem and this is Sakhnin.'

'I know. Anyway, if you don't ask, you don't get. So I'll have a go for you and you never know your luck.'

I asked Jamal why there were so few people in Sakhnin who take initiatives. Why did no one volunteer to help set up a youth club? Or to start a community centre? Or to organize volunteers to clear the rubbish?

He said: 'We have no tradition of volunteering here. None. It is very bad.'

'Well, why don't you start the tradition?' I asked him.

He shrugged: 'I did once and it worked. We got a street widened by getting all the neighbours to apply pressure and the town hall chipped in a bit. But it's really the mayor's fault. He doesn't promote initiatives.'

'To hell with the mayor,' I said. 'Why don't local people do it? Even in the area of your own *hamoula?*'

'It's not possible,' he said.

If I were a Sakhnin Arab, I would not sit still under this load of inactivity. I cannot believe that an activist could not activate.

Action, activity, change.

If I were a young Sakhnini today, I would be building from the inside. Creating communal life for young people. Or creating trouble, if I did not get the co-operation I needed.

I have never been able to endure inequality or human misery without trying, however unsuccessfully, to put right at least part of it. I deeply hated the brutal loneliness of the children in the Belsen Kinderheim, so I spent my weekends and my holidays, organizing activities for and with them. On Sundays, I gave what passed for lessons in the school, to classes of between 20–30 children, speaking a Babel of languages. I was totally unable to impose any discipline and ended up teaching by songs – the Hokey Cokey, and Underneath the Spreading Chestnut Tree – all with actions. Well, they may not have learned much but we all enjoyed ourselves. And I did at least try to help.

Part of my energy as a Sakhnini would emerge from constructive good nature. But the rest would come from anger. Someone asked Winston Churchill why he was in politics. He replied: 'I started out of ambition. I stayed out of anger.' If I were a Sakhnini, I would be angry. And I would not let that anger burn passively inside me.

Of course I would face frustration. After 18 years in opposition in the House of Commons, I became all too expert at that. But you need anger to seek its outlet.

On the other hand . . . perhaps we should be grateful at the acceptance by the community, the *hamoula*, the likes of my well-loved Shadi family, who only seek peace in their lives. 'Ah, but man's reach should exceed his grasp,' said the poet. If I were younger, I could help them to reach out and grasp. As it is, how can I help?

Jamal and I chatted about the good sides of the *hamoula* – that young people felt they had to comply with the traditional pressures, for decent behaviour. And the bad side – that the mayors promoted their own *hamoulas*.

We were joined by Jamal's nephew, an extremely well-nourished young man who laughed at my not finishing one well-stuffed pitta when he had demolished two. He was a construction worker and was always hungry and had what Jamal called 'a very big body'.

The cousin worked with Jewish people, all over the country. No problem. He and Jamal agreed that the construction industry was flourishing. People were building very big and good houses, especially in the Arab towns and villages.

Jamal said that this is what they spend their money on – houses, clothes, food and the children. So if you try to collect money for anything else, you do not get anywhere. It was not like the Jews, who chip in.

I tried to prod him into taking some initiative. He has three months' holiday in the summer, so why not use it? Useless. Swimming against the tide. Tradition. What the hell.

I wanted an ice-cream and he wouldn't let me pay for it. I had to have another drink because I was collapsing from thirst and he wouldn't let me pay for it. He said that he would be offended if I tried. So I gave up and thanked him. '*La shukr allal wajib,*' he said.

We walked up the hill towards home. The shops stay open till very late, some of them until one o'clock. I do not know when people sleep, because even the children are all awake at ten. Which is just was well, because there was a wedding on and fireworks in the air and hugely noisy music. And drivers sounding their car horns as the wedding procession arrived at the open-air canopy where the band was playing just the sort of marvellously noisy, repetitive, throbbing music that I had so enjoyed at the *ors* – the wedding which I had attended, only three days ago – three days that seemed an age.

We stopped at a shop where, after many '*ahlans*' and handshaking and '*kayf halaks*', he bought some aftershave lotion. Then we strolled back to my favourite B&B. The *hamoula* children were still awake, waiting for magic lessons, and I showed about ten of them how to palm bouncy balls. Some tried; some gave up; and all of them bounced the balls and I enjoyed the laughter as the balls leaped away and the children lost them.

Abdulalh told me that they did not want me to go. I should stay. And he and Fawzieh called me inside and gave me bottles of homemade olive oil – a big one in a grape jug, for me. A small one, in a medicine bottle, for Laura.

Chapter Nineteen

THE IMAM

Y ou can listen to a civilization. My memories of Laredo – my Spanish village – start with the sound of the newspaper boy, waking me in the morning. 'Alerta . . . Correo Español . . . Diaria Montañes.' From the sound, I see the village.

As a student at Harvard, I was woken each Thursday by an old Italian organ grinder, winding the handle and singing even before the tune emerged from his machine: 'Oh what a beautiful morning!' And so it was.

The sounds of Sakhnin? Well, you do not wake to a dawn chorus but to a couple of birds, sitting in distant trees chatting. Then there are the crickets and the doves. Otherwise, it's cars and car alarms, and children shouting and laughing.

In Laredo, we sat and sang and played guitars and drank wine. In Venice, we sat and sang and played guitars and drank wine. Here, in Sakhnin, there was the monotone Arab troubadour sound of the two singers at the wedding party on the hillside, sonorously intoning their welcomes into handheld, mouth-filling microphones, which two huge loudspeakers sent echoing across the hillsides.

More moving was the muezzin, calling the faithful to prayer. I slept through it most mornings, but today I heard it and lay and listened and thought of the few local folk who would pay any heed in this complex town, with its mixture of modern secular practice and ancient religious substructure.

They could not have the wedding party in town, because they served beer, and men and women danced together, even though they kept their bodies decently apart. The teacher of the school is a modernist and does not go to the mosque but he would not attend the party because he did not drink and did not like going to places where they do.

As wise Solomon, the police chief, told me, local lads do not shave their heads or wear ponytails or earrings, because this is an old-fashioned and decent society. But a significant few slip away and steal in other towns, where it will not affect their dignity. The traditional *hamoula* still rules, but the head of the *hamoula* does not rule the family. Their society is changing, but slowly. And hopefully, the gradual progress will not crack the ancient edifice of solid family life and religious honour.

At 7.30, I emerged from the shower and strolled with Jowdat to the family opposite. They were sitting around drinking coffee. '*Tefadal*' – they invited me to join them. A small cup of sweet coffee and half an hour of general chat.

Business is OK in the town. People are pretty contented. The children are happy. Why not?

What is it like in England? Am I happy here? How did I enjoy the wedding? They liked my dancing – and demonstrated how I had done it – rather better, I thought, than the original. Always, laughter.

Babies, crawling across the road. Vast danger, I thought. The parents shrugged. Drivers are careful. *Inshallah*.

Then Abdullah arrived and took me back onto his patio, for

supper. Salads, hummous, shishleek on skewers – overcooked – I think, because I had delayed, to speak to Nigel again, by telephone . . . Lamb chops, also cooked to death. 'So sorry.' I said. 'I've already eaten. With Jamal. But I'll keep you company.'

Over dinner, I asked Abdullah about the bill. It was back in the days of my elder daughter Marion's Chocolate Paradise, when I heard her 'negotiating' with the supplier. She was urging him to charge more, because otherwise, how would he make a living? He was telling her that she was paying quite enough already and thank you. Each was trying to get the better of the other – on the basis that what mattered was that the other did better on the deal. Finally, they settled, by splitting the difference.

I told Abdullah that I wanted the bill, please. He said: 'Next time, you pay. This time you are my guest.' I said: 'It's very generous of you. You are a very kind man. But if you do not let me pay this time, that will not be dignified and I will always be your friend and come back and see you but I will never stay again.'

He shook his head and his finger and said: 'No. You will come again and you are my guest and I will be honoured if you do not pay.' I said: 'This is your business and we had a deal and it was honourable and I wish to pay you, but I wish to pay you not only for the bed and breakfast, but also for the meals you gave me.' He said: 'No, this is your home, and you do not pay in your home.'

The conversation was getting so serious, that we talked in English. He said, finally: 'OK. But I am not prepared to accept any money from you for your lunch and dinner, where you came as my guest and we would not take money from our guests. Anyway, you make me nervous because you eat so little.'

So that was the deal. I would pay for bed and breakfast as arranged and as I was running out of Israeli money and was not prepared under any circumstances to return to the nerve-shattering bank, David or Laura would send a cheque. At which he said: 'If you have no money, I will give you some. I have money.' But I insisted and the arrangement was settled, to the satisfaction of both sides. I told him that he was a prince. He put his right hand to his heart: 'I am honoured,' he said. '*Sharaftuni.*'

Now, tell me where you will find a bed and breakfast in England where we could have the same argument? The man is wonderful and his hospitality unmatched.

He then told me that we were going off to see the Imam. Question: Does the Imam speak English or Hebrew? No. Only Arabic. Then how am I going to converse with him?

Idea: would his cousin down the street who offered to teach me Arabic come with us and interpret?

'I am sure he will,' said Abdullah. So that was that.

At 8.30, we set off in Abdullah's car. Well, 'car' is an overstatement. It is an alleged car. It is a jalopy. A wreck, which coughs and grunts and jerks along on four wheels. Every time the car stops, so does the engine. And every time we go over a bump, we shake and the car stops and the engine stalls. And as the roads in Sakhnin are made up of a series of bumps, joined together with strips of rough tarmac, riding with him is better than any fairground, but preferably not after a Shadi Guest House meal or even a felafel salad downtown.

We picked up Jamal, Abdullah's brother-in-law and cousin, who was back at his home, enjoying some rest at the end of his day. He agreed to join us, with the best of good grace, and off we went to see the Imam, who turned out to be the religious leader of the nearby village of Arraba — at least, that is what he had been. He now teaches religion in the same school as Abdullah and has handed over his job as Imam of Arraba to a less fortunate cousin.

When we arrived in the townlet of Arraba, with its 1500 or so souls, it was too early for the Imam. So we stopped at a restaurant, half way up the hill, called the Village of Peace. It was completely peaceful. The peace of the desert. Deserted. Not a living soul. A tent, with cushions on the ground. A tourist attraction, with a picture of Uzi Baram, former Israel Minister of Tourism, visiting the place. 'Delicious food', said the advert on the wall. Certainly it had a fine view and Sakhnin could do with a place like this.

Back into Abdullah's car. 'The engine needs an overhaul,' said

Jamal, gently. Indeed. And so did I.

Not only did Abdullah's car do its best to refuse to climb up the great hill of Arraba – a road as decrepit, unplanned, potholed, higgledy-piggledy and exciting as any in Sakhnin – but it had also almost run out of petrol. Somehow, after Abdullah had asked the way several times, the car staggered up what Abdullah described with his customary understatement as 'the worst road in the area', to the top – and to the home of the Imam.

Abdullah excused himself, while he coasted the car down the hill, in the hope of finding a petrol station and filling up, so that we did not have to walk home, which might have been less nerve-racking but would certainly have taken longer. Jamal and I chatted with the Imam.

The Sheikh lives in a typical local home, with comfortable armchairs around the wall and some plastic ones moved to the centre, with small tables. His wife brought fizzy orange juice, then left. With the exception of Fawzieh who occasionally sits with Abdullah and myself, the women keep themselves apart, at least in the presence of strangers.

The Imam is a bearded man of about 32. Commanding presence but no great charisma. White robe and very pleased to see us. We shoo the children away, with a handful of bouncy balls, and settle into talk.

The Imam, it transpires, speaks quite good Hebrew, so we manage between our Hebrew, my Arabic and Jamal's translation. The Imam tells us that he used to be the head of the mosque in Arraba but he found it very upsetting. People were always on his back. His sermons were either too long or too short, too filled with quotes from the Koran or without enough of them, too local and parochial or too worldly and uninteresting. Everyone had a complaint. One wanted him to talk about weddings, another about funerals . . . one about getting on with your neighbours and another about coping with the Jews.

The Imam was determined not to be involved in politics and he kept well away from that, but the stress of his congregants was too much for him. True, they did not come to him with problems at his home. They brought their anxieties to the mosque. But he had decided to hand over to his cousin, who needed the job more than he did, and he got work as a teacher in the school.

Who paid him? Well, now it was the Ministry of Education. Before, it was the Ministry of Religions. In Israel, Muslim Imams and priests and Jewish rabbis are all paid by the Ministry. Curiously, Christian priests are paid by their churches. 'But then they have lots of land and possessions and money and they are different in that way.'

I asked the Imam about the mosque being used as a centre for political influence. He agreed that it could be and sometimes was, but not here. People are influenced by the mosque, even if they do not attend. People are religious, even if they keep away from prayers. Unfortunately, most do. Still, the mosque can be a centre for political influence. But he never used the pulpit in that way.

Jamal pointed out quietly and in English that whilst this Imam was not connected to any political organization, two of the three Imams in Sakhnin were activists in the Islamist movement. 'It's not simple,' he said.

We discussed England and Sakhnin and what I was doing and we laughed at my Arabic. They all love Doug's Arab proverb: repetition can teach even a donkey. The idea that I am a donkey always pleases Arabs – and that is what I am, when it comes to their incredibly complex and (from other lips) beautiful language. I am destroying it. Or it is destroying me. We shall see which comes first.

It was by then past 11.00 and time to go. '*An ithnak*', I said. 'With your permission, I shall thank you for your hospitality and kindness. '*Illa al-liqa inshallah*' – we shall meet again, God willing. Perhaps in Britain.

Then back home, with the shaking but no longer thirsty metallic camel finding it easier to wend its way downwards through the potholes and along the highway to Sakhnin. I was glad to be home.

Then to bed. But tonight my room is at the front outside corner of the building and I shall fill my ears with those malleable ear-plugs from Warman-Freed the Chemist, Golders Green. Another world.

Chapter Twenty

FAREWELL, SAKHNIN

I packed, making sure that I had left nothing behind. Then I took my farewell presents to the living room. The family gathered. Alas, I had only two toy mice left – for the older children – I'll send two for the younger ones, very soon. Sorry. But lots of bouncy balls – they selected, each in turn. And parliamentary keyrings for all six of the family and model balloon animals for each of the children. Two donkeys, a giraffe and a dog.

Abdullah produced a wrapped, long box, which I presumed contained sweetmeats. 'For Laura and David and their children,' he said.

Shukran, shukran.

In English: 'And for you, Greevil.' A finjan – an Arab coffee pot – in bronze, inscribed: *From the Shadi Guest House to Greville Janner.'*

How wonderful.

I presented a House of Commons pill-box to Fawzieh and

cufflinks to Abdullah, and as they had given me presents they could not complain and they did not. But I still hadn't got the bill.

Will I now please sign the guest book?

'With pleasure, when I get your bill.'

He shrugged and wrote on a small piece of white paper: 800 shekels. Divide by five – that's about £160. It's £100 less than agreed – and certainly not enough. Laura and David can deal with it, when they send their cheque.

I inscribed in the guest book in Hebrew and in English that I felt at home – I was part of their family – and was very grateful. They should now come to England and let me welcome them.

I translated this for them, into spoken Arabic, as best I could.

Shukran, shukran, Greevil.

'*La shukr alla al-wajib*,' I said.

Now some photos of the family – all five of them. With my 'fun, throw-away' camera. One of the young people from the *hamoula* in a red T-shirt took one with me in it. Then I realized that we had taken the photographs with the camera that had finished its film so we took them again with the other one.

Into the back went the signed prints from the Artists' House and the photograph and plan from Gan Ner. On the floor, the pitcher and bottle of olive oil, from the Shadi Guest House. Into the boot, my well-packed brown case.

Into the front, my soft black leather hand case with the map, the dictating machines – and, above all, my precious tapes and cassettes, with my record of this visit.

Then Fawzieh produced two large paper bags. Sandwiches in one – felafel and shwarma-kebabs. Drinks in the other. 'For your journey, Jibril,' she said. 'It is a long way to Jerusalem and you must not be hungry.' Perish the thought!

A shy hug from Jowdat and another from Shadi. A handshake from the girls and from Fawzieh. A big hug from Abdullah with a kiss on each cheek. 'Follow me,' he said.

'I know the way to the road,' I said. 'This is my town now.'

'No, follow me,' he replied. So I did. The children waved once and then concentrated on the mice, the bouncy balls and the balloons. Except little Shadi, who came to my car window and said: 'When are you coming back?'

'Next year, *inshallah*. Oh yes, I'll be back.'

'Send Laura and David and the children,' said Abdullah. 'Soon.' *Inshallah.*

We wended our way down to the main road. He crossed. I waited. My phone rang. And rang and rang and rang. Where had I put it? I found it, in my black bag. It was Fawzieh. 'You've left your shoes in your bedroom.'

I pulled up alongside Abdullah, who was waiting and wondering what had happened. I told him. 'I'll go back and get them,' I said.

'No. I'll get them. You wait here.' He leapt into his car and was off. Back a few minutes later, with the shoes. Thank you. '*Shukran. Ana ajiz alla shukr* – I am so very grateful to you.'

He grinned and produced a small brown paper bag and opened it. 'Look,' he said. 'Two cups, for your coffee! Take them. They will remind you of us, your friends.'

So I left the complex, friendly, disorganized, hospitable old new world of Sakhnin. I passed Arraba and the sign for Dir Hana. Turn right for Eilabun. Past the olive groves, down the valley, with the Arab towns and villages along the road and the Jewish settlements above it. Through the timeless hills of Lower Galilee – to Tiberias, the Jordan Valley, the Dead Sea – then home, to the other world. Jerusalem. London.

Myra, where are you?

I returned the car to the hire company. 'Sorry,' said the boss. 'You did not get the wreck because you were the client.'

'It never occurred to me that you singled me out, perhaps because I am Jewish!' I replied.

'*Khas ve-khalila* – God forbid. No. It was a mistake.'

The manager came over with the account. 'Five hundred dollars, next time,' he said. I did not understand. 'You mean you're reducing the bill from 550 dollars to 500?' I asked.

'Not this time.'

'You mean that you're not making any deduction because you gave me a wreck?'

'Not this time.'

'Well, in that case, there won't be a next time.'

The boss said: 'Make it 500. Next time, come when it's not the height of the season and we'll make it 400.'

Never mind. The Cavalier was good.

I telephoned the Shadi Guest House, to thank them. Fawzieh answered the phone. 'We were so happy when you were with us. Come back. Abdullah wants to speak to you.' I thanked him.

Abdullah: 'Nothing to thank. *La shukr alla al-wajib.* Come back. Do you mind, Shadi wants to speak to you?'

Shadi: '*Tarja . . . tarja . . . tarja* . . . Come back . . . come back . . . come back . . .'

I will.

Conclusions. Hospitality, kindness, goodwill . . . and human relationships that transcend differences in culture, language and religion. A brilliant week, with delightful people. But (friends and colleagues keep asking) what are my conclusions?

Arabs in Israel – Israeli Arabs – are an unknown quantity. Unknown by their Jewish fellow citizens.

Are they a threat to the security of Israel's Jews? Fifty years without violence or unrest suggests a clear answer – no. Long may it remain so.

Are they loyal citizens? For 18 years, I was a member of Her Majesty's Loyal Opposition, desperately, continually but unsuccessfully trying to get rid of my own elected government – by lawful means. I was profoundly loyal to my country whilst seeking to undermine its government by democratic means.

I am sure that most of Israel's Arabs are as anxious as so many of their fellow Jewish citizens to dispose of their government. Arab

Members of the Knesset are at least united in that wish.

Do Israeli Arabs play a substantial role in the Middle East Peace Process? Not that I have noticed. The Arabs I met in Sakhnin were on the whole well educated, generally moderate and secularized. They should be actively involved in the search for peace. If they were, then Israel's hand would be strengthened and its image improved. Would Israel's Arabs wish to play such a role? Not, I suspect, if they are simply to be paraded as pawns in their government's game. They would need a policy role. Consultation with meaning, not simply people telling them what the government had decided.

Is the Middle East conflict still one of Arabs against Israel? Or is it now more a conflict between those on both sides who support peace, against those opposed to it?

Hamas fanatics – the suicide bombers and killers – murdered not only civilians, but also the election prospects of Israel's Labour government. Remember: terrorist killings did not begin with the Likud government. It created that government.

Did the Hamas leadership not recognize that terrorism in pre-election months would harm the Peres government, which sought peace, often in the face of bitter opposition from some of its own electorate? Of course they did. The Arab extremists still want war. They still dream of driving Israel into the sea. Unreal. But since when did fanatical extremists look to reality?

Nor did the Jewish killer of Yitzhak Rabin yearn for peaceful accommodation with Israel's Arab neighbours. He was as revolting and fanatical a murderer as any of the Arab suicidal maniacs. He, too, wished to kill the Peace Process. After his arrest, he told the world that he had to make a last second decision: did he kill Rabin or Peres? He knew he had not time for both. He killed one. His Arab counterparts destroyed the political strength and future of the other. The Peace Process faltered. The battle is between the extremists.

What, then, is the future for peace? It can only come through conversation and compromise, leading to at least a degree of mutual respect.

The people of Sakhnin, like the vast majority of their Jewish fellow citizens, want a peaceful life. To go shopping, without fear of being bombed. To travel in buses, without fear of being blown up. To travel and to live not only in democratic but also in personal bodily freedom.

The greater the hope in the past, the more depressing the disillusion as the Peace Process falters.

There is nothing new about fear and disillusion for Israel's Arab and Jewish citizens alike. There was plenty during and after the deaths by war . . . after Sabra and Shatila . . . the assassinations in the buses and shopping centres . . . the murder of Yitzhak Rabin.

Israelis – Arab and Jewish – want to live in decent peace.

I wish them and the world the conversations and the compromises, the mutual respect and understanding, without which no peace is possible.

I wish peace, to my friends in Sakhnin and to all who dwell in the State of Israel. Call it shalom or salaam – the words and their meaning are the same.

Chapter Twenty-One

REFLECTIONS

I came to learn Arabic, but learned much more. I came with one batch of questions and left with a whole lot of others.

For instance: Why don't more people do what I did?

An Israeli relative – a young woman in her early twenties – said: 'You must be joking. I'd be terrified!'

Why? the only real danger for visitors to Sakhnin are the roads in and about the town which (alas) are no more dangerous than those anywhere else in Israel. Indeed, in a lifetime of travel and political scrapes, the only dangers to my life have always been on roads and never in homes.

As a young soldier, I was sitting in the passenger seat of an army truck in Germany. The driver suddenly changed direction, throwing me against the door, which burst open. I fell onto the road and the rear wheel of the truck passed within inches of my head.

Then there was the gruesome time when the brakes gave out on my Volkswagen, on a north German hill. I held on to the wheel, literally for dear life. It careered down, with mercifully no vehicles or pedestrians getting in its way, and eventually I came to a halt halfway up the other side of the valley.

Then, the Yemen. The British Ambassador took our parliamentary group in two cars, up to the top of the Great Rift, to look down the sheer side, to the Red Sea. Unfortunately, it was a misty day and near the top we saw nothing but the road, and that was covered with mud slime.

I was in the front of the Ambassador's Land Rover, next to Mohammed, the driver. He went too fast. The vehicle skidded back and forth and slid over the edge of the cliff.

By a merciful miracle, God or Allah had created a ledge immediately below. We slid down onto the ledge . . . the wheels gripped . . . and we climbed up to the top. Our colleagues in the vehicle behind, who had watched in horror as we disappeared, leapt out and greeted us. The Ambassador exclaimed, quietly: 'As Napoleon said to his troops, you need good fortune more than skill.'

I told my Jewish Israeli family and friends: Go to Sakhnin. Do not worry about the people. But mind how you drive.

So the key political question: if Arab citizens pay the same income tax as Jewish citizens, what possible justification can there be for paying Jewish municipalities more than Arab ones?

Replies to the question included: 'Don't look for logic in this country.' 'Why do we pay more for the education of the Jewish ultra-orthodox Haredim than we do for the rest, when they neither work nor do army service?' Political pull, I suggested.

Or: 'You are right. But that is not the whole of the answer, is it? Look how marvellously Kawkab has done with its allocation? In most other cases it is the fault of the mayors . . . the *hamoula* . . . the management . . .'

Or: 'The Ma'arakh (Labour) administration was starting to put things right. And so did Aryeh Deri, Minister of the Interior, from the ultra-religious Shas party. Our new government is stopping the process.'

Shimon Peres: 'It was like that, but it isn't now. We narrowed the gap and in most respects it has gone. It is very difficult to compare as between different towns. But we did a lot to improve the position.

'For instance, I made sure that some land appropriated for military purposes was handed back to Sakhnin. They made me an honorary citizen of the town.

'Of course, it is much more difficult now. This government has not continued with the process.' The Advancement of Equal Opportunity gave me a useful pamphlet. Its content was more succinct than its title: 'Retrospect and Prospects, Equality and Integration – progress by Government Ministries in 1992–1996 in applying the basic guidelines of the Government with respect to the Arab citizens of Israel, and main objectives towards the year 2000.'

Its director, Mr Haraven said: 'Until Rabin, our Government approved a lower per capita element for Arab citizens and also less development budgets. That has changed. But there are still few Arabs in top jobs – the policy was one of containment.

'Yes, there is much to do. But do not forget the best kept secret of the State of Israel. There has been no civil unrest for 50 years. With all the problems, we have greater trouble with friction between Jew and Jew and Arab and Arab than between Arab and Jewish citizens.'

On the way to the airport with Laura my mobile rang. It was a woman called Ruth. For me. She writes for the *Jerusalem Post*, but this time she was preparing an article for the journal of the American Women's Zionist Organization, Hadassah. On Israel tourism in Arab towns. She has visited the Shadi Guest House. What did I think of it?

'Marvellous. Brilliant hospitality. Extraordinary warmth. I felt

157

like one of the family.'

'That's good,' she said. 'I spoke to Abdullah yesterday. He said that his children cried when you left.'

FINALLY . . .

I am back in Jerusalem for the Jewish New Year. Tony Blair has made me a working Labour Peer. If Myra were here to enjoy it with me, life would be excellent. Anyway, let the coming year be as sweet as is still possible, for us all.

There is a message for me. Please phone the Halayle family in Sakhnin. Shadi answers. 'Jibril, Jibril, where are you? When do we see you? We miss you. I want to learn more magic. Please come.' Then Fawzieh. 'Abdullah is out. From all of us, I wish you *Leshana Tova* – happy New Year.' Only the greeting was in Hebrew. The rest in Arabic.

I reply: '*Kul sana wa antum bekhair* – all year, may you be well.'

Fawzieh rings off. Laura, David and I discuss whether we cannot take the three children and drive up to Sakhnin for at least a day. Problems: three children, three adults, two cars. The family are in the process of trying to buy a big Volvo that seats seven, but even if they do it will be too late and an old car will go so slowly that it will take us at least four hours. Anyway, it's too far.

Abdullah phones. He tells us that the guest house is full for the New Year and is booked out for all the coming festivals. 'You know what I wish for this coming year?' he asked me.

'Tell me, Abdullah.'

'I wish that Arabs and Jews in Israel will live together in peace and as brothers.'

Amen.

I think of the big mess that Israel's government is making – most lately, that botched, mucked up, dangerous and stupid attempt to assassinate Hamas leaders, in (of all places) Amman. Plus the young people killed in an army helicopter crash. Israeli deaths in Lebanon. The suicide bombers, blasting away lives in Jewish markets, shopping malls and buses. The fanatics and lunatics on both sides. I suppose there is still some hope, when there are people like Abdullah in our world.

So I go to the *Jerusalem Post*, Israel's English language newspaper, and see the editor – Jeff Barak (né Black) – originally from Leeds. As we talk, a serious-looking man in a T-shirt, with an American accent, comes to the door. 'Sorry to interrupt. There's been a terrorist incident in Tel Aviv.'

Jeff switches on the portable radio, for the 9.30 news. The driver of a No. 5 Tel Aviv bus thought there was something suspicious about an Arab would-be passenger and asked to search his bag. The man threw away the bag, which exploded, and ran off. The bus was en route for the Dizengoff shopping centre.

Next day, the papers tell us that it was all a mistake. No explosion. We are getting paranoid.

Hayk al dunya – that is life, and death and misunderstandings and mistakes – and if they do blow off both hands, there will be no more clapping.

My seventieth birthday has just passed. My children decided on twin celebration projects. Laura is writing a collection of procedures for Jewish birth celebrations, in Hebrew, English and

Russian. In memory of Myra. And (they asked themselves then me) what else would I like best? A playground, for children in Sakhnin. 20,000 people . . . thousands of youngsters . . . no playground.

So family and friends have chipped in and both projects are on their way. A tribute to Myra, through birth and rebirth. And two hands clapping, with a project in honour of my friends in Sakhnin. *Mabruk* – congratulations, indeed.